Louis Albert Banks

John and His Friends

A Series of Revival Sermons

Louis Albert Banks

John and His Friends
A Series of Revival Sermons

ISBN/EAN: 9783337116866

Printed in Europe, USA, Canada, Australia, Japan

Cover: Foto ©Lupo / pixelio.de

More available books at **www.hansebooks.com**

John and His Friends

A SERIES OF
REVIVAL SERMONS

BY

Rev. LOUIS ALBERT BANKS, D.D.

PASTOR FIRST M. E. CHURCH, CLEVELAND, OHIO

AUTHOR OF

"Christ and His Friends," "The Fisherman and His Friends,"
"Paul and His Friends," etc.

FUNK & WAGNALLS COMPANY
NEW YORK AND LONDON
1899

COPYRIGHT, 1899
BY
FUNK & WAGNALLS COMPANY
[Registered at Stationers' Hall, London, England]
Printed in the United States

To

MY SISTER,

ADDA VARDE BANKS,

THIS VOLUME

IS LOVINGLY DEDICATED

BY THE AUTHOR.

AUTHOR'S PREFACE.

The sermons contained in this volume were delivered in the First Methodist Episcopal Church, Cleveland, of which I am pastor, in a series of revival meetings, beginning with watch-night, and continuing through the month of January, 1899. The themes had been selected long before and material gathered from time to time, but they were finally prepared, and dictated to my stenographer day by day as delivered. A very gracious revival of religion was awakened by their delivery, and a large number of persons were converted and received into the church as the result. The other volumes of this series, including "Christ and His Friends," "The Fisherman and His Friends," and "Paul and His Friends," have received such a widespread welcome not only in this country, but throughout the English-speaking world, that I am encouraged to hope that the present volume will be at least as valuable as any that have gone before it in suggestive and illustrative material, for all those who count it their greatest joy in life to win souls to Christ.

Louis Albert Banks.

Cleveland, May 23, 1899.

CONTENTS.

		PAGE
I.	—JOHN AND HIS FRIENDS,	1
II.	—THE BRIGHT HEART OF THE UNIVERSE,	10
III.	—LIGHT, FELLOWSHIP, AND PURITY,	21
IV.	—THE PERIL OF SELF-DELUSION,	30
V.	—A CONFESSING SINNER AND A FORGIVING SAVIOR,	39
VI.	—THE SINNER'S ATTORNEY IN THE COURT OF FINAL APPEALS,	48
VII.	—CHRIST STANDING IN OUR STEAD,	58
VIII.	—DOING KEEPING PACE WITH KNOWING,	66
IX.	—THE DIVINE ANOINTING,	76
X.	—A PASSING LUST BUT AN ABIDING SOUL,	88
XI.	—MEETING CHRIST WITHOUT SHAME,	99
XII.	—THE MANNER OF GOD'S LOVE,	108
XIII.	—A LOATHSOME RELATIVE AND HOW TO GET RID OF HIM,	117
XIV.	—A LOVE STRONGER THAN LIFE,	126
XV.	—THE TESTIMONY OF THE DIVINE GUEST,	134
XVI.	—THE BANISHMENT OF FEAR,	143
XVII.	—LOVE'S RECIPROCITY,	152
XVIII.	—LOVE'S EASY HARNESS,	158
XIX.	—MAN'S GREATEST VICTORY,	166

		PAGE
XX.—What is it to Live?		172
XXI.—A Prosperous Soul,		181
XXII.—The Christ in Life's Clouds,		189
XXIII.—A Candlestick in Danger,		197
XXIV.—The Hidden Manna, the White Stone, and the New Name,		206
XXV.—The Sinner's Open Door,		214
XXVI.—The Crowned Heads of the Spiritual Realm,		221
XXVII.—A Pillar in the Temple,		232
XXVIII.—The Poorest People in the World,		240
XXIX.—Christ Knocking at the Heart's Door,		248
XXX.—A Door Opened into Heaven,		257
XXXI.—The Rainbow of Mercy,		267
XXXII—Happy Wedding-Guests,		273
XXXIII.—The Great Welcome,		282

JOHN AND HIS FRIENDS.

I.

JOHN AND HIS FRIENDS.

There was at the table reclining in Jesus' bosom one of his disciples, whom Jesus loved.—*John* xiii. 23 (*Revised Version*).

JOHN is the typical man of friendship and love in that group of special disciples whom Jesus gathered round him. He stands in the world's eye as preeminently the man of heart. His gospel and his epistles and his book of Revelation are full of the rays of light and love, and abound in descriptions of conversations with the Master which are full of the very marrow of divine tenderness.

While Christ loved all of his disciples, and indeed loved all men, with a heart overflowing with sympathy and compassion, there were, as Morley Punshon has aptly commented, distinctions among the apostolic band. Three of them, Peter, James, and John, seem always to have been selected on the great occasions which stand out most prominently in the life of our Lord. They seem to have been the innermost circle round the Master, the nearest in intimacy, the most favored in fellowship, the chosen ones to testify to any special revelation of his love. Their very names, Dr. Punshon suggests, were significant of the great purpose for which Christ came into the world: that the "gift or mercy of God," founded upon a "rock" of impregnable strength, stood to "supplant" all idolatry and error. When the power of Christ over death was to be displayed in the weeping household of the ruler of the synagog whose little daughter had faded into the still beauty of the tomb, Peter and James and John were the only witnesses selected by Jesus to behold her miraculous recovery. On the Mount of Transfiguration, when the inner glory of the Savior's nature burst forth in wondrous beauty, or in the mystery of the agony in the Garden of Gethsemane, this same trio of faithful and loving men were selected to accompany their Lord.

In these three men Christ secured three distinct characters. James, the earliest apostolic martyr, was as stedfast and constant as the everlasting hills. Other men might forget their devotion, might give way to panic in the face of unexpected opposition; but no one ever dreamed of James doing a thing like that. He could die, but he did not know how to run, or to be other than faithful to his vow. In Peter, there was the impetuous, ardent advocate. True, he denied his Lord, and left that blot forever on his name, but he came back to his fidelity with as much impetuosity as he had shown in his desertion, and forever after was the outspoken, daring mouthpiece of Jesus Christ. John, the Greatheart, "the disciple whom Jesus loved," was the supreme type of intelligent affection. He seems to have come closer to Christ than any one else. While Peter was always the first to act, John was ever the first to know the mind of Christ, and to perceive the presence of the Lord. On that morning when the little company had been at sea all night, fishing without success, and as the day dawned they beheld Christ on the shore, it was John who first knew him, and said, "It is the Lord." Peter was the first to act on this information, for he impetuously sprang overboard and swam ashore. And in this historic scene connected with our text, the same characteristics in the two men come out. Christ had just told them that one of them sitting with him at the table would betray him. With wonder and sorrow each man questions, timidly and tremblingly, "Is it I?" Then Peter makes a sign to John, who is reclining in Jesus' bosom, that he should ask Christ who it is, and John whispers in the ear of Jesus the question and receives the whispered answer in reply.

I think it is well for us, at the very beginning of this month of special consecration to the worship of God, in which we shall seek with definite purpose to win our fellow men to yield their hearts to

Christ, to remember that our religion is supremely a religion of the heart. The life of Jesus is a life of friendships, a life of personal relationships, and we have constantly suggested the fact of his love for different individuals, and his delicate and generous appreciation of their love and gratitude in return. Jesus rejoiced to have people do things for him because they loved him; and if we are to please Christ perfectly in this month of revival effort, it will be because we gain spiritual strength by reclining in his bosom, and go forth to win men to him for love's sake.

This truth is beautifully illustrated in the story of the woman who came to Christ when he was at dinner in a rich man's house, and washed his feet with her tears, and wiped them with the hairs of her head. The host was angry at the sight, and, greatly disgusted, thought within himself: "This man, if he were a prophet, would have known who and what manner of woman this is that toucheth him: for she is a sinner"; and no doubt he thought that word "sinner" with a sneer of contempt. But his thoughts were not hid from Christ. Jesus saw the sneer and the thought that was behind it, and answered the man's silent contempt by saying: "Simon, I have somewhat to say unto thee. And he saith, Master, say on. There was a certain creditor which had two debtors: the one owed five hundred pence, and the other fifty. And when they had nothing to pay, he frankly forgave them both. Tell me, therefore, which of them will love him most? Simon answered and said, I suppose that he to whom he forgave most. And he said unto him, Thou hast rightly judged. And he turned to the woman and said unto Simon, Seest thou this woman? I entered into thine house, thou gavest me no water for my feet; but she hath washed my feet with tears, and wiped them with the hairs of her head. Thou gavest me no kiss; but this woman since the time I came in hath not ceased to kiss my feet. My head with oil thou didst not anoint; but this woman hath anointed my feet with ointment. Wherefore I say unto thee, Her sins, which are many, are forgiven."

Surely that incident must have been recorded for the purpose of forever setting beyond all cavil the fact that Jesus Christ rejoices in the personal love of his friends, and that service is glorified in his eyes when it is done for love's sake. How ashamed we ought to be of ourselves when we go about our Christian work as though it were a load to be carried, and not a joyous privilege. Is it not quite possible for us to go to church every Sunday morning and Sunday night, and attend the prayer-meeting regularly and give a regular sum to support the Gospel, and yet so imitate Simon in the formality and coldly critical spirit of our service that when the hour is over and we have gone home, our Lord could say to us truthfully: "You gave me no kiss, you did not anoint my head with oil, you gave me no water for my feet; you bowed your head in prayer-time, you put your money in the contribution basket, but you gave me no loving overflow of tenderness and gracious services"? God save us from such a comment from him who hesitated not to give his own life on the cross for us!

When we come to enter into fellowship with John, the Greatheart, we find that we can not enjoy our own fellowship with Christ without sharing it with others. John's big heart always had room for somebody else. Christ knew this when, as he hung on the cross, he gave his mother into John's keeping. And he who comes to love Christ finds that his own spiritual joy depends on sharing it with others.

During the last great famine in India, one of the missionaries in the famine district had just seated himself with his family at the dinner-table, and they had begun to eat, when they were interrupted by a peculiar noise on the veranda. A boy and a dog were fighting over a bone. The boy was so thin and emaciated from long-continued hunger that his ribs could be plainly counted under the skin. The dog was almost as thin and hungry as the boy; and the bone they were fighting over was one that had been thrown away by the missionary's servant after every particle of meat and even marrow had been removed from it. The missionary called his wife, and she and the children came running out. The dinner was forgotten in the presence of that terrible sight of human misery.

"We never can enjoy our dinner, John," cried the missionary's wife, "as long as such a thing as that is going on within reach of us!"

The boy and the dog were separated, and the boy was cared for in the missionary's home; but no one wanted to sit down to the table in that house until that awful condition of human suffering was relieved. They could not enjoy their own meal with the vision of that savage scene coming up before their minds.

If we are truly the Lord's, the sight of spiritual hunger and famine will appeal to us, and it will not be possible for us to enjoy our own feast of love with Christ unless we are conscious that we are doing our very best to bring the bread of life to these other perishing souls. It is a terrible thing that we should sometimes seem to be so indifferent to the men and women who are dying of spiritual famine—people whose hearts are breaking in sorrow without the knowledge of Him who is our soul's greatest comfort; men and women who are chained by wicked passions, who are held in cruel bondage by evil habits; and yet we, who have learned the song of jubilee, who have been given freedom by the great Deliverer, are so timid and hesitating about making known the opportunity of freedom to these who are held in such bitter bondage! I pray God that the Holy Spirit may give us eyes to see clearly the sad ravages which sin is making upon the unconverted people whom we know, and that we shall so appreciate their needs that in self-defense, for our own joy's sake, our hearts shall prompt us to bring salvation to them.

It is only heart-religion that can give us that sympathetic atmosphere which will help us to win souls. A friend was asked: "What is the secret of Wilberforce's success?" "In his power of sympathy," was the ready answer. He was large-hearted, generous, and liberal; he went straight to the front, and threw himself heart and soul into every project which had good for its object. It was said of Norman Macleod that sympathy was the first and last thing in his character—he found in humanity so much to interest him; the most commonplace man or woman yielded up some contribution of humanity. "When he came to see me," said a blacksmith, "he spoke as if he had been a smith himself; but he never went away without leaving Christ in my heart."

We must not hold people at arm's length with some cold intellectual reasoning if we would win them to Christ. We must think about their condition, must meditate on their need of Christ, must muse on the transformation that would come if they knew Jesus; must pray about them, carrying their personality before the mercy-seat, until our hearts are filled with the longing to see them Christians; then when we go to talk with them, the heart-fellowship of sympathy and love will make itself felt, and will be more powerful than anything we say or do to make the Christian life charming to them.

We must not be too particular as to whom we shall win. Any man, woman, or child who does not know the Lord will seem infinitely desirable to us when we look at them through the light of Christ's love and sacrifice in their behalf. George Macdonald says a man must not choose his neighbor; he must take the neighbor that God sends him. In him, whoever he be, lies hidden or revealed a beautiful brother. The neighbor is just the man who is next to you at the moment. This love of our neighbor, he says, is the only door out of the dungeon of self. What a glorious month it would be for us if this first month of the new year should liberate every member of this church from the dungeon of selfishness, and grant unto us that indescribable joy that comes to those who are conscious of having been the instruments, in the hands of God, of bringing liberty and forgiveness to a soul perishing in its sin! Such a happy privilege is within the reach of every one of us. God grant that we may seize the opportunity, and each become a Greatheart in the enthusiasm and love with which we give ourselves to winning souls for the Master!

II.

THE BRIGHT HEART OF THE UNIVERSE.

This is the message which we have heard from him, and announce unto you, that God is light, and in him is no darkness at all.—*1 John* i. 5 (*Revised Version*).

THE supreme duty of a Christian minister is set forth with perfect clearness in this text. According to John's idea, the minister is the messenger of Jesus Christ to announce to his fellow men the truth about God. He is not to formulate his own message; he is not to bring them the results of his own philosophizing or theorizing; he is to bring to them the message of his Master. What Christ says about God is the great substance of the message which the Christian minister is to announce to the people. That was what Paul meant when he said at one time, on coming to a people, that he should know nothing among them save Jesus Christ and him crucified. To Paul's mind, the great sacrifice of Jesus Christ on the cross as an atonement for the sins of men was the essence and substance of the revelation of God's heart to the world, and it was therefore the substance of Paul's message which he was sent to announce to the people. I do not understand that there has been any change in the order of the Christian ministry. Men are not called of God to be mere theorizers about the Gospel, but are called to announce the Gospel itself; not to make a Bible, but to declare one already made. We are called not to declare the vaporings of our own imagination, but to point to Christ, the Savior of the world, and call sinners to repentance before that God who is light, and in whom "there is no darkness at all."

It is a very happy and cheerful message which I have for you this morning—a message of good cheer for every one. My message is that the Heart of the Universe, the Center from which shine forth strength and wisdom and beauty, is bright and full of all radiant things, and that in that great and glorious Center "there is no darkness at all." If a man is ill, there may be more or less gloom over the household, and many fears and forebodings among anxious relatives; but if I can find the physician, and know that in his mind there is a perfectly clear conception of the case, and that he has no doubt whatever of his ability to deal with it, or of his power to banish the disease and bring the patient speedily back to health, then my confidence is at once restored, and the fears of those who do not understand the case no longer make me anxious. It is good cheer like that which I bring to you this morning. This world of ours is sick with sin; it has been covered with strife, and torn by war and pestilence and famine. Sin stalks abroad yet, sometimes like an epidemic, but always working in secret, preying upon the hearts and lives of men and women, ever and anon sending forth defiant shouts of fiendish victory from its strongholds. Many people become frightened and discouraged, and believe that mankind is getting worse, and that the human race staggers like a man sick unto death to its grave. Many are the moans and the hopeless cries of despair, until one is depressed by all this mingled sin and sorrow which meet the gaze on every hand. But to every one who has come under such an influence I have a message of good cheer. I have it from the very mouth of Christ, who came forth from the Father, and who speaks with knowledge, that in the heart of God there is not now, nor has there ever been, any sense of discouragement. His heart has ever been full of hope and courage. No darkness of fear or doubt or anxious foreboding has ever clouded the divine Mind. He has seen the end from the beginning, and has known that all these things which have discouraged us are but temporary, and that goodness is infinitely stronger than evil, and is yet to triumph among mankind. In the bright Heart of the Universe there is no fear that mankind will collapse in its effort toward righteousness and stumble back like a drunken man into the darkness. God sees always that man's way is upward; and Christ, looking forward past the cross on Calvary, past the grave in the garden of Joseph, past the Mount of Ascension, past our day and beyond, saw the travail of his soul, and was satisfied with the glorious victory that he was to win in the hearts and souls of men.

Knowing that God is not discouraged, and that he expects victory, ought to encourage our hearts and give us that power of expectancy in which lies victory.

One of Spurgeon's students said to him: "I am afraid I have mistaken my calling, and that the ministry isn't my proper work."

"Why," said Spurgeon, "what is the reason you have come to that conclusion?"

"Well, I have been working in such a place for such and such a time, and I don't seem to have accomplished much."

"Why, man alive! you didn't expect that every time you preached a sermon somebody would be converted, did you?"

"No, of course I didn't expect that."

"Well, you don't get it, then. Expect results, and you will find them."

This great message which John brings to us from Christ, that there is never for a moment any sense of discouragement or defeat in the heart of God, and that he is able to conquer every wicked habit and heal the heart of every sin, ought to illuminate our own souls, and give us faith and courage to expect great things in our efforts to save sinners.

It should comfort us very much to feel that there is no darkness of ignorance in the mind of God. He is not taken unawares by any unexpected troubles that confront us. Unforeseen as they have been to us, and unprepared as we may be to meet them, God has not been taken by surprise, for in him there is no darkness at all. He has known all about it, and thoroughly understands the case now, and has not a single dark cloud of foreboding concerning the outcome. This thought ought to lead us to trust God perfectly and have no anxious fears.

A little four-year-old inquired of her mother one moonlight night: "Mamma, is the moon God's light?"

The lamp had just been put out, and the timid little girl, as well as her mother, was afraid of the dark; but presently she saw the bright moon out of her window, and it suggested the question, "Is the moon God's light?"

"Yes, Ethel," replied the mother; "his lights are always burning."

Then came the next question from the little girl: "Will God blow out his light and go to sleep too?"

"No, my child," replied the mother; "his lights are always burning."

Then the timid little girl gave utterance to a sentiment which thrilled the mother's heart with trust in her God: "Well, mamma, while God's awake I am not afraid."

We may be sure that there is no darkness of ignorance or drowsiness at the Heart of the Universe, which is forever bright with the wakefulness of abounding love.

There is no darkness of prejudice in the mind and heart of God. What an evil track prejudice leaves behind it in this world! One often hears a complaint that this one or that one has not had a fair chance because the people who had the power to control to some extent his destiny were prejudiced against him. God is never prejudiced against any of his children. Prejudice is always born either of ignorance or sin, and neither of these has any place in God's heart. There are no dark jealousies or envies or prejudices in the bright heart of our Heavenly Father. There could not be false testimony enough heaped together in the whole world to prejudice our case before him for a single moment. He knows everything about us; he sees every purpose that is formed in our hearts; he knows what we strive to do just as well as what we actually succeed in accomplishing. No soul will ever be shut out of a fair chance, for in the brightness of God's countenance are perfect knowledge and perfect justice. And if any soul cries out in its anguish, "Perfect justice will mean my condemnation forever, for I have sinned against God," then take heart, "for God so loved the world that he gave his only-begotten Son, that whosoever believeth in him should not perish, but have everlasting life. For God sent not his Son into the world to condemn the world, but that the world through him might be saved."

In this month to come it will be our special duty, not only from the pulpit, but from the pew, day after day to announce to every man and woman and child within our reach Christ's message concerning God—his brightness of goodness and love, and his perfect knowledge and hatred of sin. There is so much of this glorious light of God in his Word that if we will speak it to people with loving earnestness it will illuminate its own pathway to their hearts. It is not for us to defend the Word of God, or argue about it, or speculate about it; but with complete self-surrender to obey it and announce it to others.

It is related of Dr. Cæsar Malan, that once, meeting an infidel in the streets of Paris, to every one of his sharp assaults he simply responded by quoting a text of Scripture, and saying, "Thus saith the Lord." "But," said the Frenchman, "I don't believe it." "Nevertheless," answered the faithful man, "it is the Word of the Lord, and if you don't believe it you will be damned." Years afterward the same man met Dr. Malan, and after reminding him of the occurrence, said: "It was that which convicted me. You did not let me get hold of the hilt of the sword and begin to examine and criticize it, but you thrust the sharp point of it right through me every time, and it wounded me to death, and also to life eternal." And so it will be in our hands. "For the Word of God is quick, and powerful, and sharper than any two-edged sword, piercing even to the dividing asunder of soul and spirit, and of the joints and marrow, and is a discerner of the thoughts and intents of the heart." This is so because the bright presence of God in the Holy Spirit is in the Word to give it power.

We are all called to this glorious work of bringing the brightness of God to dispel the darkness which sin has brought into the world. The call is to every one of us. Great results await on our united and earnest cooperation. It is not only to feel right about it, and have good wishes and cordial sympathy for the effort that is being made to promote religious revival; it is the actual putting of our own shoulder to the burden, the becoming ourselves messengers to announce this heavenly good cheer, which is required of each of us. I have been reading again that song of Deborah and Barak with which they celebrated the victory over Sisera. In that song particular condemnation is meted out to the tribes of Reuben, because, altho they were very friendly, and talked very kindly and cordially, when the time of battle came they were not found on the battle-field. This is the way it is described: "For the divisions of Reuben there were great thoughts of heart. Why abodest thou among the sheepfolds, to hear the bleatings of the flocks? For the divisions of Reuben there were great searchings of heart." Thus it is that they were held up to contempt for their miserable emotions and their "searchings of heart," which were, however, never strong enough to get them out of hearing of the bleating of their own sheep. Alas! the tribes of Reuben still have their representatives in the world. Dr. Watkinson tells of a boy who came into an English library the other day and asked for a book for his mother. He said she wanted one to make her cry. Exactly. There are lots of people that like to read books that stir up their emotions and arouse their tender sentiments; but they never go out to help the poor, or visit the sick, or reclaim the drunkard, or win back the sinner from his sin, notwithstanding all their tears. There is something very insinuating in Deborah's song about the Reubenites. "Why abodest thou in the sheepfolds to hear the bleating of the flock?" No doubt they could have given her fifty reasons why they did not go to battle, but she suggests as a reason that they were cowards. They stayed in the sheepfold because they were selfish and indolent, and cared more for looking after their own flocks than for the exertion and risk of battle, even tho it were for a worthy cause. Their brethren were suffering oppression, and to be left in the lurch at such a time might prove their overthrow; but these sheepherders stayed at home and listened to the bleatings of the lambs while the din of battle was going on.

We are going to battle in this church. There is need for every man, woman, and child connected with the church to be on hand, with every ounce of influence and force that they have, to carry on this battle against sin, and to present to those who have it not the bright and glorious Gospel which has been committed to us. In this hour I am praying that there shall be no Reubenites among us. Let there be no one who shall be so taken up with business, or pleasures, or any other selfish interests, that he shall refuse to come out daily to the help of the Lord against the mighty. This is a battle in which mere good wishes will not avail. It is your presence we want; it is your prayers; it is your personal appeals to the unconverted; it is your testimony for the Lord; it is you, yourself, with every weapon that God has given you or that he is willing to give you, that we need in this fight. There will be some sick ones who can not come, and some that are too aged and weak to come; but God save us from having lazy ones and self-indulgent ones who stay at home to hear the bleatings of the flocks while their brethren are in a life-and-death struggle to save immortal souls from eternal bondage to sin!

It is a glorious opportunity that we have. "He that winneth souls is wise." "He which converteth a sinner from the error of his way shall save a soul from death and shall cover a multitude of sins." These souls that Satan is holding in bondage are the jewels of God, and it is our opportunity to rescue them to shine in his crown forever. The time soon passes, the opportunity will soon be gone; but it is ours now. Let us work with all our might while the day lasts, for the night hastens when no man can work.

III.

LIGHT, FELLOWSHIP, AND PURITY.

But if we walk in the light, as he is in the light, we have fellowship one with another, and the blood of Jesus his Son cleanseth us from all sin.—*1 John* i. 7 (*Revised Version*).

MAN was born for the light, and must have a bright atmosphere in order to come to his best. There are some species of life that belong to the gloom and grow rank in the darkness; they seem to revel in a black, cheerless atmosphere; but man does not belong to that grade of life. Man is of so high an order of being that his soul faints within him in the darkness. We are the children of God, and in order to develop our true life we must walk daily in the light of God's countenance.

A great deal depends upon the atmosphere in which one lives. A manufacturer of carmine, who was aware of the superiority of the French color, went to Lyons and bargained with the most celebrated manufacturer in that city for the acquisition of his secret, for which he was to pay five thousand dollars. He was shown all the process, and saw a beautiful color produced; but he found not the least difference in the French mode of fabrication and that which had been constantly adopted by himself. He appealed to his instructor, and insisted that he must have concealed something. The man assured him that he had not, and invited him to see the process a second time. He minutely examined the water and the materials, which were in every respect similar to his own; and then, very much surprised, said, "I have lost my labor and my money, for the air of England does not permit us to make good carmine." "Stay," said the Frenchman, "don't deceive yourself. What kind of weather is it now?" "A bright, sunny day," replied the Englishman. "And such are the days," said the Frenchman, "on which I make my color. Were I to attempt to manufacture it on a dark, cloudy day, my results would be the same as yours. Let me advise you always to make carmine on bright, sunny days."

This story of the carmine manufacturers strikingly illustrates the difference between a life, however moral and upright it may be, which owes its morality purely to hereditary tendencies or the restraining influences of public sentiment—a life which is manufactured, so to speak, in the cloudy, gloomy atmosphere of human selfishness, without any reference to God, from no love or gratitude to him—and the same morality which is woven into life in the light of God's countenance, where deeds of uprightness are performed in an atmosphere of prayer and thanksgiving and loving self-sacrifice.

The first brings no sense of joy, and is colored with none of the romance of the immortal life. That which gives the Christian life its glow of heavenly color is the bright and glorious atmosphere in which it is produced. The radiant beams of the Sun of Righteousness fall upon it; the light of immortality floods it; and the hope of heaven, the prospect of eternal reunion with loved ones, the promise of likeness to Christ, animate the Christian character with divine energies, and give a color to the moral character of the Christian that surpasses anything that can be produced in a merely worldly atmosphere, however cultured or refined it may be.

The man who lives in the bright atmosphere of God's presence can not walk in darkness. If we turn our faces away from God, then every step brings us toward the deep darkness. No doubt some who hear me are ready to say with Tennyson's Rizpah: "The night has crept into my heart and begun to darken mine eyes." If you get night into your heart, you are certain to get darkness for your eyes. But there is no night for the heart that suns itself in the light of the bright heart of Him who is light, and in whom there is no darkness at all. That is a remarkable expression in Paul's letter to the Ephesians in which he uses the phrase, "Having the eyes of your heart enlightened." Blindness in the physical eyes is sad enough, but it is a small matter compared with blindness in the eyes of the heart. If the heart does not see God, it is a lost heart, a dead heart, a despairing heart. To such a heart God will seem vague and unreal or cruel. To a blind heart the Bible seems dull and beyond understanding. But when the eyes of the heart are opened they behold God's beauty, the loveliness of his character, the brooding tenderness of his patient and persistent love seeking after lost souls, and the indescribable mercy which provided redemption for ruined men. I would to God that every blind eye of the heart might be opened here to-night, so that you should behold with clearness the repulsive character of sin, and the beauty and loveliness of God's mercy in Jesus Christ!

We have suggested in our text a thought of fellowship—a fellowship both human and divine. It is promised that if we walk in this bright atmosphere which radiates from the heart of God we shall have fellowship one with another. That is, we shall see heart to heart in a sweet and precious brotherhood; we shall be in close touch with all others who walk in this same light of God, and whose hearts, like our own, are in harmony with the bright heart of the universe. It is not our outward fellowships, but our inward spiritual fellowships, which will dictate our eternal destiny. You remember the story of Dives and Lazarus which was told by our Lord and recorded by St. Luke. While here in this world, Dives was surrounded by the most luxurious circumstances, and was no doubt the object of the jealousy and envy of a great many people. He dressed in apparel fit for a king, and dined on the most sumptuous viands that money could procure. But Dives, instead of using his wealth and his great opportunities to bless the world, allowed the luxury in which he lived to narrow and harden his heart, and to make him selfish and mean in his attitude toward others. To his eye his poorer brothers were fit only to be companions for dogs, and he thought he did well to permit the crumbs from his table to be flung to them with contempt. The fellowships of his soul were hard, unfeeling spirits like his own. But near by was another man named Lazarus. He lived at the other extreme of worldly condition. He was poor, he was a cripple, he was covered with loathsome sores, and his outward fellowships were confined to the street dogs; and yet, despite all these cruel outward conditions, the man by some marvelous spiritual alchemy retained his self-respect, and lived in heart-fellowship with that which is highest and holiest. Dives, in the midst of all that was outwardly beautiful and refined and luxurious, developed that which was mean and low and ugly and devilish in his nature; while Lazarus, surrounded by all that was ugly and impoverished and repulsive, developed within himself a rare and beautiful spiritual nature. So when the curtains of earth are drawn aside and the earthly houses fall to pieces—one on a couch of down and the other on the stones of the streets—at the gate of the mansion there is a wonderful transformation scene. Dives leaves his beautiful robes behind, to live forever after in the vile rags of his sins; while Lazarus leaves his rags behind, to be clothed upon forever with robes of light and dwell in fellowship with princely natures like Abraham. Where are your fellowships? I don't ask you whose parties you go to, on whose visiting-list you are found; but where are the fellowships of your soul? Are they with the friends of Jesus Christ, the people who love God and are seeking to walk in the heavenly way? Or are your fellowships with those who forget God, who are careless of his law, and who render no loving testimony to Jesus Christ?

Then we have the thought of purity. That is the supreme result of all. "If we walk in the light, as he is in the light, we have fellowship one with another, and the blood of Jesus his Son cleanseth us from all sin." The light of God's heart, the life produced in this cheerful atmosphere, the fellowship with the holiest, is to lead us to that perfect surrender to Jesus Christ which will result not only in the forgiveness of all our sins, but in the cleansing and purifying of our hearts, so that we shall do God's will out of wholesome, loving natures. Let us make no mistake. Walking in the very light of God's countenance will not save us. Satan walked there once, and yet through his pride and rebellion fell to the lowest hell. There is no power in the walking or in the light to save us. We may have the closest association with Christian people in daily fellowship, and yet die in our sins. Judas walked in close fellowship with Christ and his disciples for years, and was a trusted officer among them, and yet died the death of a traitor and a suicide. No; there is no salvation save in the atoning blood of Jesus Christ. We have sinned against the law of God, and because of our sin we are already under condemnation. If we were to turn over a new leaf right now, and never sin again, we still would not dare to face the Judgment Day, for the sins that are back of us would cover us with everlasting confusion and sink us in the blackness of despair. Our hope is in the fact that Jesus Christ came to the earth of his own accord, and was born under the law, took upon himself our flesh, and, after being tempted in all points like as we are, died the death of the cross in our behalf. When we repent of our sins and believe on Christ as our Savior, God transfers our sins to Christ's account, and we are forgiven.

We are not only forgiven, but cleansed and renewed. We would still be helpless if there were no change in our moral nature, which has learned to love that which is sinful. But when we take Jesus Christ as our Savior, God by his divine Spirit adopts us into the inner circle of his children. He takes away the hard heart and gives us a heart of love and gratitude. The old sins which we once loved we now hate. Our moral nature becomes healthy and normal, and we worship God and serve him in the loving spirit of childhood.

I know that I speak to-night to many who are saying in their hearts: "It would be a glorious thing if such a transformation could come to my heart and life; but it is too good to be true." Do not, I pray you, allow the enemy of your souls to deceive you in that way. It is good enough to be true, and it will be true, if you will obey Christ at this time. I know there is something in your hearts that answers this appeal. There is an old legend that in the valley of Eusserthal, in Switzerland, where are the ruins of a convent choir, there was once a golden organ that stood in the church and was played during divine service. When the convent was attacked, the first care of the monks was to save this treasure; and they dragged it to a marsh and sank it as deep as they could. The old legend holds that it is still in the neighborhood, though the spot has never been found, and that it sometimes rises out of the swamp at midnight, and its sublime tones are heard in the distance. Nothing is comparable to the gentle breathings of the golden pipes in the solemn stillness of the night. At such times the soft tones swell into mighty billows of song which rush along the valley and die out at last in echoes through the forests. So the harmonies of the noble and pure life that was seen in Jesus Christ belong by right to every one of us. In some of you they have been buried deep beneath selfishness and sin; but you have moments of memory and vision when, rising up out of the swamp of worldliness in which you have drowned your better self, you catch sweet tones of hope and love and faith. I know that you have midnight hours of penitence and aspiration, when you loathe your sins, and when the Christ-life seems infinitely beautiful and appears very near and possible to you. May this be one of your vision hours! May the Holy Spirit so enlighten the eyes of your heart that this noble life in Christ Jesus may seem possible to you now; and may you rise up and respond to this appeal which comes to you through the mercy of God!

IV.

THE PERIL OF SELF-DELUSION.

If we say that we have no sin, we deceive ourselves, and the truth is not in us.—1 *John* i. 8 (*Revised Version*).

It is hard to conceive of a more pitiable state than to be self-deluded in a matter of great importance. It is sad to see a man who has struggled and toiled through all the strong years of his life to gain a competency and to lay by something for old age, and who has believed that his investments were so made that his fortune was secure and his resources abundant, find, when it is too late to remedy it, that he has been deceived, and that all the earnings of his years of toil have taken wings and flown away, and that the apparently secure investments were only frauds and delusions. It is sad to see a man whose health is being undermined by an insidious disease, the ravages of which are apparent to his friends and acquaintances, but the victim himself deluded into believing that he is in no danger; that he is indeed on the high road to recovery, and will soon be well again. Who of us has not known of such cases, where up to the very day of death this self-delusion continued? But it is sadder yet to see a man deceived about his soul; deluded into believing that he has no need of a Savior, while in truth he is living every day under condemnation of the broken law of God. Sad to see a man going onward toward eternity, spending all his energies on this world, which he is hastening to leave, and laying up no treasure in the other world, in which he must spend the eternal years.

Christ tells us that in the great Day of Judgment there will be people sadly aroused from their delusion—people who will point back to their life in this world, and tell with what ostentation they performed religious ceremonies while here on earth, and with what pious emphasis they spoke of Christ, and what deeds of charity they did in his name; and yet shall hear the startling and awful words: "Depart from me; I never knew you!" It is a terrible thing to be awakened from a delusion when it is too late for remedy. If we have sins, in God's name let us know it now, while by the grace of Christ we may be forgiven of them and rid of them.

The central theme of our meditation this evening is surely this, that there can not be any possible self-justification on the part of any man or woman in the world. If we are saved in heaven at last, it will not be because we were so good in ourselves, but because of the divine mercy bestowed upon us. There is not one of us who will dare to plead that we have kept, not only in deed, but in thought and in motive, always, on every occasion, the entire law of God. There is not a day passes but the truly enlightened and sensitive soul feels the need to pray for divine mercy and forgiveness. Christ related to his disciples the story of two men who went up into the temple to pray. One of them was proud of his morality. He was very self-complacent about himself. He was careful to keep all the outer ceremonies and conditions of the law. He even went so far that he fasted twice a week and gave tithes up to the last dollar of all he possessed. And when he came to prayer it was with the spirit that he was rather a subject for congratulation than for divine mercy. He thanked God that he was not like other people, especially that he was not like this poor sinner, the publican, who had come into the temple at the same time with himself. He asked for nothing; and why should he, when he seemed to be all-sufficient in himself and had no consciousness of need? The other man was in a very different mood. In many ways he was not so good a man outwardly as the Pharisee. He was a sinner. His wicked life had brought him under the condemnation of God and man; but something, we know not what, had brought him to his senses. It may be that his sins had become so flagrant that they had brought him into shame and disgrace. It may be that great sorrow had come to him through the death of some of his dear ones, and he suddenly saw the folly of his sin and the utter worthlessness of anything save goodness in the great emergencies of life. Or it may be that in the very midst of his sinful career his conscience suddenly aroused and rebuked him, and the still small voice of the Holy Spirit spoke to his inmost soul as it did to Elijah in the mountain-cave, saying, "What doest thou here?" And in that sudden awakening of his conscience he thought of the temple as a fit place for him to go; and coming into that holy place, his sense of unworthiness came over him with such oppression that he knew not what to say, but in his agony and contrition he smote with his hand upon his guilty heart and cried, "God be merciful to me a sinner!" And Christ says that it was this man, and not the other, who found justification through his prayer.

Some people make the fatal mistake of measuring their lives against the lives of their neighbors, and delude themselves in that way. A man compares himself with some acquaintance who is a member of the church and whose conduct is inconsistent with the Christian profession. This neighbor comes far short of the opportunities and privileges of the Christian life. And so this self-righteous moralizer thinks within himself: "If that man gets into heaven, surely no just God will shut me out." Thus he lulls himself to sleep, not because he has faced the sins of his own heart and sought forgiveness, but because he has measured himself beside a poor sinful fellow man and come to the conclusion that he is better than his neighbor. It looks too silly to be possible, and yet many people are deluding themselves in just that way. The foibles of your neighbor have nothing to do with you. You will never be judged in comparison with your neighbor. You will be judged on your own conduct, as to whether you lived up to the light which was given you. Suppose a man were brought before the court to-morrow morning accused of swindling, and he should plead as a justification: "Judge, I know I got money dishonestly, that I obtained goods under false pretenses; but surely you can't blame me, at least you can't condemn me, when you remember with what a dishonest set of people I live. Why, I can point out a dozen men on the same block, every one of whom is worse than I am." Do you think that would be any extenuation for the prisoner's crime? You know it would not be. He must stand and give answer for his own sin. And so it is with you. Every man must give an account of himself before God. And when you come to do that, in your sober, honest moments you know that it is not justice, but mercy, which you will have to crave.

Mr. Spurgeon tells of a man who was discovered, with a gun and a dog, trespassing on private grounds, and who said that he was only looking for mushrooms. The keeper could not imagine what a gun and a dog had to do with mushrooms. So he felt in the man's pockets; and laying hold of something soft, asked: "What is this?" "Oh," said the poacher, "it's only a rabbit." When it was

THE PERIL OF SELF-DELUSION. 35

suggested to him that the creature's ears were too long for a rabbit, he said it was only a leveret; but when it was pulled out of his pocket it proved to be a very fine and plump hare. The man then said that he had found the hare lying near the mushrooms, but his intention was to get the mushrooms only. So, Mr. Spurgeon says, as soon as ever you lay hold of a man and begin to accuse him of sin, he says: "Sin, sir! Oh, dear, no! I was only doing a very proper thing, just what I have a perfect right to do; I was only looking for mushrooms." You press him a little more closely, and then he says: "Well, perhaps it was hardly the thing; it may have been a little amiss, but it was only a rabbit." And when the man can not any longer deny that he is guilty of sin, he says that it was only a leveret, a very little one. And it is long before you can get him to admit that sin is exceedingly sinful; indeed, no human power can do that—it must be the work of the Holy Spirit. May the Holy Spirit do his office work in the hearts of those who are deluding themselves into the belief that they have no need of forgiveness, no need of God's pardon, no need of conversion, while all the time they are under condemnation; and who, if they should die to-night, would be eternally lost! How much better to awake to your sin now, when you may turn from it to Christ and be forgiven, than to delude yourself until you shall join voice with that company who shall cry for the rocks and the mountains to fall upon them and hide them from the face of the Lamb!

Our theme to-night ought to impress upon us the folly of trusting in any outward religion to take the place of the inner cleansing of the heart by the blood of Christ. There is a story of a Nova Scotia sailor who has the Lord's Prayer tattooed on his back. He says that his dying mother asked him never to part with the back cover of a family Bible, on which the Lord's Prayer was printed in letters of gold. For many years he carried this cover on all his cruises; but one day, having a tussle with a sailor, he lost it overboard. Bad luck pursued him after that; and finally a companion who had heard him lament the loss of the talisman suggested his having the prayer tattooed on his back. He did this, tho he suffered very much during the process. Alas! there are many who are making the mistake of this poor, ignorant, superstitious sailor. There are multitudes who are putting their religion on the outside rather than on the inside. The Lord's Prayer can not do any good on a man's back, but it may lift him up to fellowship with angels if it be engraved on his heart. It is your heart that God asks for, and nothing else can possibly satisfy him. He has given you every good thing that you have, and he has given heaven's best for your redemption; and only by your love, only by giving him yourself in return, can you put yourself in such an attitude toward God that your sins may be

THE PERIL OF SELF-DELUSION. 37

forgiven and he may bestow upon you the joy and glory of sonship.

Some of you have been throwing your influence on the other side for a long time. The silent testimony of your daily life has been against Christ. If you were to change about to-night and come out openly on the Lord's side, and give your Savior the benefit of that testimony, no one is able to measure the good you might do. Dr. Munhall was once holding services in a large town. He was told that the most prominent business man there was an infidel. He was a man of intelligence and morality, but a very pronounced opponent of religion, who missed no opportunity of denouncing Christianity and its professors. To the surprise of Christians, he attended the first meeting of the revival. They soon found, however, that he came to mock. The sermon that night was on "The Heinousness of Sin." He went away seriously thoughtful. He came the next night, and Dr. Munhall preached on "God's Remedy for Sin." He remained to pray, and went home a saved man. So overwhelmed was he with the consciousness of the great debt that he owed to God and his neighbors, that he closed his place of business for the entire two weeks during which the meetings continued, and visited from house to house, apologizing to the people for having ever advocated infidel views, and assuring them that the religion of Jesus Christ was a sublime reality. He told them of his own conversion, and urged every one to attend the meetings. Many came on his invitation and were saved. Some of you who hear me to-night, if you were to forsake your sins now and find pardon in Jesus Christ, might do glorious work in the next few weeks in winning others to the Savior. Do not stay away; do not let Satan deceive you about yourself; do not delude yourself by any false confidence; but come humbly to the mercy-seat, and throw all your sins and cares on Jesus, who died to redeem you.

V.

A CONFESSING SINNER AND A FORGIVING SAVIOR.

If we confess our sins, he is faithful and righteous to forgive us our sins, and to cleanse us from all unrighteousness.
—*1 John* i. 9 (*Revised Version*).

CONFESSION of sin to God is simply being honest and genuine toward God. The ostrich, which when closely pursued in the desert thrusts its head into the sand, and imagines because it has closed its own eyes it is therefore safe from its pursuer, is not more unreasonable than the man or woman who undertakes to hide sin from God. God is never deceived for a moment. There is no darkness in his mind, and every thought and purpose of our daily lives are open unto him. The story of Ananias and Sapphira is a very clear illustration of the folly of trying to deceive God. When the disciples voluntarily sold their private property and brought it and cast it into a common fund for the support of the early church, Ananias and Sapphira his wife were in a quandary. They were selfish, greedy people, and yet they wanted to stand well before the other disciples; and so they sold their property and put half their money away in secret, and brought the other with great show of generosity. But Peter, by the aid of the Holy Spirit, saw their wickedness and their lie to God. And Peter said: "Ananias, why hath Satan filled thine heart to lie to the Holy Ghost, and to keep back part of the price of the land? Whiles it remained, did it not remain thine own? How is it that thou hast conceived this thing in thy heart? Thou hast not lied unto men, but unto God." And Ananias, hearing these words, fell down and gave up the ghost. And a few hours after, his wife, not knowing of the discovery of their sins, and not having learned of her husband's death, came to Peter, and he asked her: "Tell me whether ye sold the land for so much. And she said, Yea, for so much. But Peter said unto her, How is it that ye have agreed together to tempt the Spirit of the Lord? Behold the feet of them which have buried thy husband are at the door, and they shall carry thee out. And she fell down immediately at his feet and gave up the ghost: and the young men came in, and found her dead, and they carried her out and buried her by her husband."

We do not wonder that Luke should add: "Great fear came upon the whole church, and upon all that heard these things." But the same thing is happening to-day all around us. The judgment of God does not always come so suddenly, but multitudes now are perishing because they are hiding their sins and are dealing falsely with God. Men delude themselves into believing that in some way their own evil nature, for which they think they are not responsible, or the temptations of Satan have been too strong for them, and therefore they could not help doing what they have done. There is no greater delusion than that. We have the power to refuse admission to the evil one, for all the angels of heaven are at our call if we ask help of God. In this story of Ananias and Sapphira, which I have recalled, Peter recognizes that Satan has filled the heart of Ananias with lies, but he does not hold Ananias any the less responsible on that account, for the devil could never have entered the heart of that greedy man if the door had been shut against him by prayerful resolution. The question that meets Ananias and Sapphira face to face is: "Why hast thou permitted it?" We can not escape from our sin by throwing it off on the devil. The devil can do nothing with us if our hearts are true to God. He has no power to compel men to do his bidding until they have yielded themselves of their own free will to become his servants. If it is true of you now, as was said of one of old, that you are "led captive by the devil at his will," then it is because you have yielded your own neck to the halter. When the devil undertook to compel Christ to turn from the path of right, Jesus said of him: "The prince of this world cometh and hath nothing in me." The devil could make nothing out of

Christ because every pulsation of Christ's heart was true to God. We can not escape from our sins by throwing them on the devil; we can not put them off on our neighbors; we can not thrust them upon any fault in our own nature; they are our own sins. In spite of all the will power that God gave us to fight the world, the flesh, and the devil, and all the power that he offers to us to bring us off more than conqueror, we have admitted the enemy of our souls into the fortress of our hearts.

There is no more terrible and awful deception ever practised by Satan than to convince men that sin is all-powerful, and that they can not help but yield to him. When the Spaniards invaded Mexico, Cortes sought to make the Mexicans believe that a Spaniard could not die, a deception which utterly unnerved them in the day of battle. But God's Word is full of the records of victory over temptation and sin; and a man is lost who gives himself up to the belief that he is the devil's slave and can not help it. Society is full of men and women who are daily winning glorious battles over temptation and sin. Magnificent moral victories are being won on every hand. As Dr. Watkinson aptly puts it, we see the ugly side of life; if anybody goes to the bad, we all know it. But all around us are sublime spectacles of moral heroism and victories over the evil one which would inspire us with exultation if we could see everything that is going on. Here is a young man who has the cup of guilty pleasure pressed to his lips, but in the critical moment on which hangs eternity he dashes it to the ground. Here is a young girl who by the grace of Heaven turns away from some alluring cluster, keeping her purity and her paradise. Here is a struggling young business man who prefers honesty to gold, or a politician who loses an election rather than lose self-respect. Thank God! the devil does not always get the best of it. There are innumerable men and women who by God's grace walk the muddy pathways of life with unspotted robes.

No, your sin is not somebody else's; it is your own. Bad as it is, ugly as it is, loathsome as it is, it is charged against your soul. There is only one way to escape it, and that is to drag it to judgment at the mercy-seat, and have it forgiven. It is a glorious promise we have to-night. "If we confess our sins, he is faithful and righteous to forgive us our sins, and to cleanse us from all unrighteousness."

To whom shall we confess our sins? First of all, to God. Your sin is against God. It may be that it is against man also. It is easy to conceive of cases where it will be necessary to confess sin to our fellow men. If you have wronged any one and sinned against him, the moment you have made your confession to God you will feel the justice and propriety of going at once and confessing to this person. It may require restitution on your part; if you have wronged any one in a way that restitution is possible, then you never can have peace until you have done your best to make it right.

How can I confess to God? As I said in the beginning, the essence of confession to God is honesty and genuineness about your sin. You have been trying to hide your sin, not from your neighbors only, but from your own heart. Stop doing that. Think about your sin. Meditate upon it now as I talk; let your memory bring it back and hold it up before your gaze. Oh, I know it is not a pleasant subject to think about, it is not a pretty picture to look at; but you had better look at it now than look at it in the Day of Judgment, when the opportunities of forgiveness and salvation have passed forever. Recognize your sins yourself. Confess them now in your own heart; say over now in your thought: "I am a sinner against God."

As soon as you begin to recognize your sin and confess it to yourself, you will feel drawn by a deep current of impulse to make some public confession of it to God in the presence of your fellow men. You have been sinning in the presence of your fellow men, you have been living your indifferent and selfish life before the world; and it is surely most appropriate that you should seek to put yourself right, and make a public confession of your change of attitude toward God and toward the Lord Jesus Christ.

The very moment you make this public confession you come into a new atmosphere, a new realm of promise, and you are able to claim this pledge: "He is faithful and righteous to forgive us our sins." This is a very strong, very significant sentence. The whole philosophy of the atonement made for us by Jesus Christ is wrapped up in this text. God does not forgive us, when we confess our sins, as a mere act of favoritism or mercy. It is a deed of justice and righteousness. If you owe a debt and are not able to pay it, and I am your friend, and, coming to know your distress, I volunteer to go and pay the debt for you, it is only just and right that you should be discharged from the debt. Now this is the way the case stands with our salvation. We were poor, lost sinners; we were hopelessly lost and bankrupt, and had nothing whatever to pay. But in spite of our sin God loved us and longed for our salvation. And so when we had nothing to pay, and there was no friend to redeem us, he devised the wondrous plan, a plan beyond all human philosophy and thought, by which Jesus Christ, the Divine Son, came out from the Father's heart, and, putting aside the glory of heaven, came down to earth and undertook to ransom and redeem us. In order to do it he must become one of us, so he was born in the manger at Bethlehem; he tasted all the weakness and sorrow of our flesh; he toiled in the carpenter's shop with the laborers; he was tempted by the devil in all points as we are; he was lonely; he was treated rudely; he was crowned with thorns; he was spit upon and insulted, and finally he was crucified on the cross, that he might, in the red drops of his own life-blood, pay the debt of our sin against the broken law of God. I am not here to explain it all to you. I do not pretend to understand it all. I only know that there is in it a divine alchemy by which a poor, lost sinner, weighed down and oppressed by his guilt, may, if he will, lay his sins down at the foot of that cross, and know that those sins are forgiven; may feel that his burden is rolled away, and realize through all his ransomed and redeemed nature the thrill of a new life of hope and love as the forgiven son of God.

Men may mock it and sneer at it as they will, but the only hope for a sinner in this world or any world is in the divine and blessed fact that Jesus Christ came into this world to save sinners, and that he died on the cross for their redemption. Men may sneer at the blood of atonement and count it an unholy thing, but it is the pulsing blood of eternal life, and it is the only hope for lost sinners. Our hearts ought to melt within us as we look on the cross of Christ and see there the sacrifice that made it possible for God to be faithful and righteous and yet the forgiver of our sins. I would to God every unconverted soul here might have those two looks that John Newton had, about which he sings with such tenderness:

A SINNER AND A SAVIOR.

"I saw One hanging on a tree
   In agony and blood,
Who fixed his languid eyes on me,
   As near the Cross I stood.

"Sure never, till my latest breath,
   Can I forget that look;
It seemed to charge me with his death,
   Tho not a word he spoke.

"Alas! I knew not what I did,
   But now my tears are vain;
Where shall my trembling soul be hid?
   For I the Lord have slain!

"A second look he gave that said,
   'I freely all forgive;
This blood is for thy ransom paid;
   I die that thou mayest live.'

"Thus while his death my sin displays
   In all its blackest hue,
Such is the mystery of grace,
   It seals my pardon, too!"

VI.

THE SINNER'S ATTORNEY IN THE COURT OF FINAL APPEALS.

If any man sin, we have an Advocate with the Father, Jesus Christ the righteous.—*1 John* ii. 1 (*Revised Version*).

THERE can be no doubt that this is an interesting text for every one of us. It refers personally to our own case. If it had specified a certain class of sinners, then the rest of the world might have been uninterested. If it had specified rich sinners, or learned sinners, or people of any special grade or class in society, it would have shut the rest out. But this declaration is as broad as human life. "If any man sin." That means me, and it means you. Who is there here to-night that will be willing to stand up and say: "I have never in all my life sinned against the law of God. I have in my inmost heart, as well as in my outward life, kept faithfully all his law"? I am sure there is no one here ready to make such a statement as that. It means every one of us.

And what a glorious thing it is that every poor sinner, no matter how friendless and alone he may be in this world, has an equal chance with the richest and most popular man on the earth in the services of this great Advocate, who offers to stand and plead for him before the high court of heaven! We hear it often said that the poor man who has neither money nor friends has a poor chance to get justice in the courts, provided he is fighting against some rich and powerful person or corporation. But there is one court where that is not true, for the greatest Attorney in the universe stands ready to plead in behalf of the most friendless sinner who seeks his services. Indeed, his heart is so great in its tenderness that I am sure he bends lower to catch the cry of the weak. Isaiah, looking down to this day of the Gospel and of Christ's interceding love, says it shall be a time when "the lame take the prey." Charles Wesley in one of his greatest hymns embodies the same thought in the closing verse:

> "Lame as I am, I take the prey,
>   Hell, earth, and sin, with ease o'ercome;
> I leap for joy, pursue my way,
>   And as a bounding hart fly home,
> Through all eternity to prove
> Thy nature and thy name is Love."

In the worldly struggle a man who is lame in any way misses the prey, and is at a great disadvantage in the fierce competitions of life; but in God's dealings with us it is different. He has the heart of a father, and Jesus Christ, our Advocate, has the heart of the ideal, tender, loving brother, and just because you are weak and frail and feel your weakness the great Advocate will give you his most devoted service. Dr. Meyer says he was one day staying in a farm-house. With one exception the family consisted of robust, hearty children; but there was one little lame boy. There came in a great hamper of apples, and at once all the boys and girls in the family, having eyed them wistfully, proceeded to appropriate, and to appropriate very lavishly, the apples. The little lame fellow, with his puny, wan face, looked forward eagerly as those apples disappeared, and no one thought of him till the mother came, a bustling, quick-tempered woman. She said: "What is that you are doing? Put all those apples back again, I tell you." And very ruefully they replaced them. "Now," she said tenderly, and her voice took on a new tone of gentleness as she spoke, "Jimmy, you come and take your pick." And the little lame fellow hobbled on his crutches up to the table and, encouraged by his mother, took the ripest and juiciest, and filled his pockets as full as they would hold, and then hobbled back with a flush on his pale cheeks. Then the mother said to the other children, "Now you can do what you like with the rest." It was easy to see that in the mother's love the little lame boy took the prey. Brother, sister, you that are discouraged and feel that you are too weak and sinful to undertake this high and holy life, let me urge upon you with all my heart that never mother loved her little crippled child with a love as deep and comprehensive as that which Jesus Christ feels for you, and never for any fee did lawyer work as hard as the Divine Advocate will plead for your soul if in your weakness and your sin you turn to him for help.

I am not preaching to you any vagary; I am preaching to you something that you may test for yourself. This is no agnosticism. Do not, I beg of you, be drawn off by any such folly as that. Some one has well said that the religion of "don't know" is a very poor article for any man to keep on hand. You ask such a man if there is a personal God, and the answer is, "I don't know." If there be such a God, what are his attributes and his relation to men? "I don't know." Has a man a soul distinct from the body that dies? "I don't know." If he has a soul, will that soul survive the event of death and live forever? "I don't know." Is there a heaven and a hell? "I don't know." Is the Bible true? "I don't know." Was there a Jesus Christ who came into this world to save sinners? "I don't know." Did Jesus Christ rise from the dead and ascend into heaven, and does he now exist there as the Intercessor and Savior of sinners? "I don't know." God have mercy on the man who is compelled to answer all such questions in that way! Such a man would do well to examine the ground on which he stands. He declares his own ignorance upon the most important questions that can be asked or answered. No others are or can be to him of so much importance; and yet he dismisses them all at sight by simply saying, "I don't know." This is the one saying which he flings at every religious truth, and with which he seeks to relieve himself from its pressure. Ah, the real secret is that the man dare not face his sin and does not want to know. The devil deludes him into preferring the religion of "I don't know" rather than that of "I do know." But, my friend, when you come to die, if you have your reason in that solemn hour, you will not be satisfied with the religion of "I don't know." Then your soul will cry out for some certainty upon which to rest itself. Then you will long to know something which contains the solution of what death is and is to be to you. You will find it a difficult task—ah, indeed, an impossible task—to get out of this world in peace on the naked theory of "I don't know."

You may know, and you may know now, that this great Savior who offers to be your Advocate at the throne of mercy is true. He has promised that if you will take his word and do the first duty that is at hand you shall have light to shine through your darkness. Dr. Arthur Pierson says that once in Detroit, one Sunday night after preaching, he invited any one who might desire to do so to meet him in another room to converse about personal religion. On entering the room he found there one young man. He judged him to be about thirty years old; he was stalwart-looking and intelligent, and would have been fine-looking but for a cloud that seemed to abide upon his countenance. In fact, his face seemed scarred and furrowed, as tho he had been through a life battle with sin and care, and had been terribly worsted in the contest. Dr. Pierson said to him: "I take it, sir, that you are here to talk with me about your spiritual interests. If so, will you at once let me into the very heart of your trouble? I am acting as a physician to souls: let there be perfect frankness between us, and I will do anything I can for you."

"Well, sir," said he, "I suppose you would consider my case a desperate one. I am a follower of Ingersoll. I am an unbeliever, an infidel."

"But I suppose there are some things you believe. You believe the Bible to be the Book of God?"

"No, sir."

"You believe Jesus Christ to be the Son of God?"

"No, sir."

"Well, at least you believe in a God?"

"There may be a God; I can not say I believe there is, but there may be; I do not know."

"Then let me ask why you are here. I can not waste time and words to no profit. I hope you have not come here to trifle with me. And yet I do not see what you want of me if you do not believe in the Bible nor in Christ, and are not even sure there is any God."

The young man replied: "I have heard you preach to-night, and it seems to me that you must believe something——"

"You are quite right, I assure you," Dr. Pierson interrupted.

"And it seems to me," continued the young man, "that it gives you peace and comfort."

"Right again!"

"Well, I don't believe anything, and am perfectly wretched, and if you can show me the way to believe anything and get happiness in believing, I wish you would."

"I understand you," replied the Doctor, "and I would risk my own salvation, if necessary, upon yours, if you will follow my prescription."

Dr. Pierson bowed his head a moment in prayer, and even while he prayed the young man at his side broke out again with an exclamation: "If you can do anything for me, I wish you would. Can't you tell me something to read?"

"I would have you read nothing but the Bible. You have been reading too much; that is partly what is the matter with you. You are full of the misleading, plausible sophistries of the skeptics. Read the Word of God."

"But what is the use of my reading the Bible when I do not believe it to be the Word of God?"

Dr. Pierson opened his Bible and read: "Search

the Scriptures, for in them ye think ye have eternal life, and they are they which testify of me."
"Now," said he, "if that means anything, it means that he who diligently searches the Scriptures will find that they contain the witness to their own divine origin and inspiration, and to the divinity of the Lord Jesus Christ."

"Well," said the young man, "I'll read the Bible; but what besides?"

Again turning the leaves of the Bible, the preacher read: "Enter into thy closet, and when thou hast shut thy door, pray to thy Father which is in secret; and thy Father, which seeth in secret, shall reward thee openly." "If that means anything, it means that if you sincerely pray to God he will reveal himself to you."

"But, of what use to pray to God if you don't believe there is a God?"

"It makes no difference," replied Dr. Pierson, "provided you are sincere. If it be only feeling after God, if haply you may find him who is not far from every one of us; if it be only like

>"'An infant crying in the night,
> An infant crying for the light,
> And with no language but a cry'—

God will not disregard any genuine effort to draw near to him. Go and pray, if only like another in your case, 'O God, if there be a God, save my soul, if I have a soul.'"

"Anything more?" said he.

"Yes." And the Doctor read again: "If any man will do his will, he shall know of the doctrine." "That means that if you act up to whatever light you have you shall have more light. In God's school we never are taught a second lesson till we practise the first."

"Now," said Dr. Pierson, "I have given you three texts already to ponder and study. I wish to add one more: 'Come unto me, all ye that labor and are heavy laden, and I will give you rest.' That means that if you come directly to Jesus, he will give you rest. Now notice these four texts. One bids you to search the Scriptures; one, to pray in secret; one, to put in practise whatever you know; and the last, to come to Jesus as a personal Savior."

"Is that all?" he inquired.

"That is all. Will you promise me to go and follow this simple prescription?"

"I will."

After kneeling in prayer together, this follower of Ingersoll left him. Two weeks later, at the close of the sermon, the same young man came almost running toward him, with both hands extended and his face beaming as he said: "I have found God and Christ, and I am a happy man!"

Then he told Dr. Pierson the fascinating story. He had gone home that Sunday night, taken out from his trunk the Bible his mother had put there when he had left home; had opened it and knelt before the unseen God. He simply, sincerely asked that if there were a God at all, and if the Bible were the Word of God and Jesus Christ his Son and the Savior of man, it might be shown him plainly. And as he read and prayed and sought for light, light was given; he humbly tried to follow every ray and walk in the light, and the path became clearer and plainer and the light fuller and brighter, until his eyes rested in faith upon Jesus.

I have told you this long story because it has in it the throbbing of a man's heart who through darkness sought after Christ by taking him at his word, and found him the true Advocate he had promised to be. Follow his example to-night; it is action that you need; do the duty that is next to your hand; confess Christ here and now, and trust him to fulfill his promise.

VII.

CHRIST STANDING IN OUR STEAD.

He is the propitiation for our sins; and not for ours only, but also for the whole world.—*1 John* ii. 2 (*Revised Version*).

OUR message to-night is very plain and very comforting. Our sins have broken the law of God and have brought us under its condemnation. It would not be possible for God to sustain moral government in the universe unless some one made satisfaction for this sin. It does not impugn God's love to say that. A ruler and a judge may be compelled to sentence a prisoner directly against the love of his heart. If law is to be maintained, it will often lead to a conflict between law and love. We have an illustration of this in the story of David. Absalom had slain Amnon and fled to Geshur, and there remained in banishment for three years. David loved Absalom with all his heart, and the writer of the history says that the soul of King David was consumed with longing to see his favorite son again. Love would have restored him, but law forbade his restoration. The father in David cried out for the sight of his son and for his reinstatement at court, but as a king he was responsible for the administration of law. He was compelled to keep Absalom in exile, banished from his own presence at the very time when his heart was consumed by the tender love he felt toward him. Our sins have brought about exactly the same conflict between law and love in the heart of God. It is idle and wicked for men to speak of God's punishment of sin as if it were cruel and vindictive. The universe would be full of anarchy and ruin were there not a just God on the throne who enforces law without respect of persons.

I think these reflections make it very plain to us that the only hope of escape from bearing the just penalty of our sins is in some one from the outside, who is not under the penalty himself, some one great enough and good enough and who loves us enough to come and stand in our place and suffer the penalty in our stead. The same thought is illustrated in the proposition which Judah made to Joseph in the court of Pharaoh in Egypt, when Joseph proposed to keep Benjamin as a hostage. Judah said: "Now, therefore, I pray thee, let thy servant abide instead of the lad a bondman to my lord; and let the lad go up with his brethren." His proposal was that he should stay in Benjamin's stead and as his substitute. So in his infinite love God gave Christ to be bondsman or surety in our place, and Jesus willingly laid aside the glory of heaven and came and stood in our stead. To propitiate is to satisfy. Our sins had offended the law of God, and Christ came to satisfy the broken law which condemned us. He came to take our burden of sin on his own shoulders and bear its penalty.

What a new element that introduces into the words by which we often close our prayer, "for Jesus' sake." We have no standing at the mercy-seat except in the name of Jesus.

Not only on the cross did Christ take your place, but now, in your sorrow for sin and in the remorse of your guilty conscience, if you will open your heart to him and confess him before men, he will come and take your place within your own heart. He will take away the stinging sense of guilt and condemnation and leave there his own perfect peace. Dr. Reginald Campbell, an English preacher, tells how, on one occasion, he was sent for to see a lady, a stranger, who was dying in Brighton. He found her to be a woman of wealth and education, but quite ignorant of the leading facts of the Christian faith. Her religious views had been formed almost entirely by the influence of certain Oriental cults. To her Jesus was simply a great moral teacher, standing in line with other religious masters. Of Christianity as the religion of redemption she had no knowledge. Her life-story had been a sad one, stained deeply by both sorrow and sin. The poor suffering soul stated it for herself in words that are charged with meaning. "Oh," she sighed, "that it were possible for some great strong friend to take my conscience as tho it were his own, that I might have a little peace!" Dr. Campbell said that he learned more from that sentence concerning the mystery of redemption than up to that moment he had ever thought of. Here was a soul who knew and stated the need of just such a salvation as we are bidden to proclaim. She asked, without knowing that there was any answer, for the Savior who was made sin for us, who came to stand in our stead, who could take man's conscience as tho it were his own and leave in its place his peace. The sense of guilt had awakened with power in this poor dying woman. To have told her, on this last day of her life, that the Most High could forgive her sins would have carried no comfort to her heart. The only possible relief for her was to hear of Him on whom the Lord hath laid the iniquity of us all. And is not that your need tonight—that this great and glorious Friend of sinners, who died in your stead, and who was raised from the dead for your justification, shall come and take your guilty conscience and give you his peace?

Do not fail to notice that this plan of redemption has its source in God's love. The record says, "The Lord hath laid on him the iniquity of us all." There is a hymn which says,

> "I lay my sins on Jesus,
> The spotless Lamb of God";

but, as another has well said, we have no power to

do that. We can not lift one sin from ourselves, much less lay it on Jesus. We can simply lay our sins at Jesus' feet and cry:

> "Thou who hast borne all burdens, bear our load;
> Bear thou our load whatever load it be;
> Our guilt, our shame, our helpless misery;
> Bear thou, who only canst, O God, my God,
> Seek us and find us, for we can not thee."

God takes our sins, and himself lays them on Him who was smitten for our transgressions. "For God so loved the world that he gave his only begotten Son, that whosoever believeth on him should not perish, but have eternal life."

Do not, I pray you, lose out of sight the personal character of this sacrifice of Christ. It was for you. It was for us. "He is the propitiation for our sins"; "He was wounded for our transgressions, he was bruised for our iniquities." Never forget that it was your sins that thrust that cruel crown of thorns upon his sensitive brow; your transgressions that caused the nails to be driven through his hands and feet; your wicked imagination and impure heart that thrust a spear into the Savior's side; your sins that bore down with crushing weight on his soul until, heart-broken, he cried, "It is finished."

Do not turn away from this salvation because it is so simple and easy. Thank God that the way is open for every man, and that the weakest and poorest may come. Mr. Moody tells of a man who was converted in Europe several years ago, and he liked the Gospel so well he thought he would go and preach it. He started out, and great crowds came to hear him just out of curiosity. The next night there were not so many there, and the third night he had scarcely a hearer. But he was anxious to preach the Gospel, and so he prepared some great placards and posted them all over the town, declaring that if any man in that town who was in debt would come to his office before twelve o'clock on a certain day with the proof of indebtedness, he would pay the debt. This news spread all over the town, but the people did not believe him.

One man said to his neighbor, "John, do you believe this man will pay our debts?"

"No, of course not; it's only a hoax."

The day came, and, instead of there being a rush, nobody appeared.

Now it is a wonder that there is not a great rush of men into the kingdom of God to have their debts paid, when a man can be saved without money and without price.

Well, along about ten o'clock, a man was walking in front of this new convert's office. He looked this way and that, to see if anybody was looking, and by and by, satisfied that there was no one, he slipped in, and said:

"I saw a notice about town that if any one would call here at a certain hour you would pay their debts. Is there any truth in it?"

"Yes," said the man; "it is quite true. Did you bring the necessary papers with you?"

"Yes."

After the man had paid the debt he said, "Sit down, I want to talk with you," and he kept him there until twelve o'clock. Before twelve o'clock had passed two more came in and had their debts paid. At twelve o'clock he let them all out. Some other men were standing around the door.

As the three came out, they began to ask, "Well, did he pay your debts?"

"Yes," they said; "it was quite true; our debts were all paid."

"Oh! Then we'll go in and get ours paid."

They went, but it was too late. Twelve o'clock had passed.

It is an offer like that that Christ makes to you and to every sinner in the world. He says: "Him that cometh to me I will in no wise cast out"; "Come unto me, all ye that labor and are heavy laden, and I will give you rest." His invitation is not to people that are already fairly moral and upright, but to sinners of every sort and kind; "He is able to save unto the uttermost all that come unto God by him." To every sinner who stands bankrupt before the law of God—and every sinner in the world is thus bankrupt—Christ is saying, "Come unto me, and I will pay all your debts."

And you have abundant evidence that Christ is

able and willing to do what he offers. The noblest and holiest men and women that have ever lived have borne happy testimony that Christ had power to make peace between their souls and God; power to take the sting of guilt out of their consciences and fill their hearts with joy unutterable. Every day adds to the number of those who accept Christ and find that he is able to do everything that he has promised. Come yourself and test him to-night!

VIII.

DOING KEEPING PACE WITH KNOWING.

And hereby know we that we know him, if we keep his commandments. He that saith, I know him, and keepeth not his commandments, is a liar, and the truth is not in him: but whoso keepeth his word, in him verily hath the love of God been perfected.—*1 John* ii. 3–5 (*Revised Version*).

CONDUCT is the best evidence of character. Conduct is to character what leaves and flowers and fruit are to a tree. Conduct tells the kind of spiritual tree that is growing within. Doing should ever keep pace with knowing. No man will ever be condemned for not doing a duty that he did not know about, unless his ignorance came through his own wickedness. But every one of us is under obligations to God to live up to all the light we have. There is a very stern Scripture in regard to those who know what is right and yet do not do it. Jesus says that the servant who knows his Lord's will, and does not act on his knowledge, "shall be beaten with many stripes." Knowledge is always a serious and responsible thing. A man can never act as if he did not know. Knowing our duty puts upon us the obligation to do it.

The essence of our truth to-night is that religious knowledge and desires and impulses are of no avail whatever unless they crystallize into conduct. The important question is not how much truth you know, but how much of it are you living? There have been many men who knew more than enough truth to have insured their salvation, and yet they were lost. There have been those who had many good impulses and desires, and who fondly imagined that they would be among the saved at last, and yet through failure to put their good impulses into conduct they died in despair without God and without hope.

The Bible gives us many conspicuous examples of men who have come to believe in God, and have come to know their own sins, and who have confessed their sins; and yet, failing to act up to their knowledge in seeking forgiveness and entering upon a new life of righteousness, it has all gone for naught, and they have died wicked men. Pharaoh rebelled against God, and refused to give freedom to his slaves, until the hail spoiled his harvests, and the thunder rocked the heavens, and the lightning burned the forests, and his heart died in him for fear. Then he sent for Moses and Aaron, and confessed that he was a sinner in the sight of God. He admitted that the Lord was righteous in his conduct, and entreated Moses to pray for him that the thunder and the lightning and the hail might cease, and promised to let Israel go. But when the sun shone again, and the air was full of the joy of the morning, and all was quiet and peaceful, he hardened his heart against God, and refused to keep his word. Then the locusts came and covered the land, and everything that had been left by the hailstorm was being devoured. Pharaoh again yielded to the cry of his people and to the fear of his own heart, and called Moses. Again did he confess his sin and beg the servant of God to intercede for him, and promised to obey God. But when the locusts were gone he forgot his promise, and was as hard-hearted and cruel as ever. Then the darkness fell over the land of Egypt, the thick darkness that could be felt. And in the horror of that hour again Pharaoh relented, and yet again returned back to his sin. Then in the midnight the death angel passed over Egypt, and in every Egyptian house was a funeral. The first-born of every household lay dead, from the hut of the poor to the palace of the king. And while the wailing of dirges were going up on every hand, and the whole land was draped in mourning, Pharaoh rose up in the night, and not only let the children of Israel go, but, proud monarch that he was, begged that they might bless him as they went; and yet, after all this, he did not really repent, but hardened his heart against God, and followed after the children of Israel in wicked rebellion against Almighty God, until he miserably perished with his army in the sea. There never was and there never can be a man with a better chance to repent than Pharaoh had; there never was a man who sinned against more light; but he sinned against it all, and was lost. He had had many hours when he was moved to do right and to serve God, but he never got beyond that fatal point of indecision and never surrendered his heart and life fully to God.

Balaam is another striking illustration of a man who knew the truth, who knew his duty, and who had many hours when he wanted to do it, and yet who tried to serve God and serve Mammon too. He wanted to enjoy the money of wickedness and at the same time escape the curse of God. When the angel of God blocked his path and sought to turn him back from his evil way, he confessed that he was a sinner and declared that he was willing to do what God wanted of him. But he tried to walk on both sides of the road. He wanted to save his soul, but he was determined to have money even if he lost his soul. There is never any doubt what will happen in a case like that. He lost his soul. He died on the battle-field, fighting for the enemies of God. No man ever went down to hell in his sin who knew his duty better than Balaam. He was a brilliant man. The path of duty was as clear as day to him, but he did not act up to his light. All his knowledge and all his good impulses went for nothing, and he died unsaved.

Judas is another signal illustration of how a man may live in the midst of Christian people, may have Christians for his friends and daily associates, may hear the Gospel daily for years, even from the very lips of Jesus himself, and yet through failure to put his knowledge into practise may die only in the greater and deeper despair because of the brightness of the light against which he has sinned. Now in each of these three cases—and I might multiply them without number—the light was abundant. Each of these men was convicted of sin again and again, was so deeply convicted that he publicly confessed—sometimes with anguish and breaking heart—"I have sinned!" And yet they were all lost. Each one died in his sin. I pray God that none of you may follow their wretched example!

I have known men and women who were deceived by the devil into the belief that it could not be possible that they could be lost because their consciences were so tender, and they were so often sorry on account of their sins. I have had a man say to me, "I never do wrong but what I am at once sorry for it." But, my dear friend, there is no virtue at all in that. That is only an indication of God's goodness toward you, and not of yours at all. Pharaoh had that experience; it was Balaam's chronic condition; Judas felt that way, but it did not save them from becoming so deeply the slaves of sin that they rejected God until the last, and died in despair. I don't ask you how much conviction of sin you have to-night. I am not inquiring into how many good desires or good impulses fill your breast. I am not asking how tender your heart is, or how much sorrow you have when you have done wrong; I come as God's messenger to your soul to ask you: Are you doing your duty; are you obeying God's commandments; or are you, in spite of all your light—from your own conscience, from the Bible, from the pulpit, from your mother's prayers, from your Christian rearing—in spite of it all, are you daily living in rebellion against God, refusing to confess Christ before men, and going step by step on the downward way that leads to death?

The Bible has other illustrations of men who came to know their sins and realize them, and acted very differently and with happier results. I will only call your attention to one of them—the one in the story of Christ where there is a father with two sons; and one of them is a restless young fellow who frets against the restraints of home, and begs his father to give him his part of the inheritance and let him go into a far country and seek his own fortune. The father is sad about it, no doubt, but the young man is grown, he must judge for himself, and so the father deals generously with him and bids him a broken-hearted farewell. In the far country everything seems to go his way for a time. He squanders his money upon the friends that are always ready to gather round the prodigal and the spendthrift. He resolves to have a good time, and for a while in the wild whirl of passion he is intoxicated with the pleasures of sin. But it soon passes by. The devil's pleasures are expensive, and before long the bottom drops out of his pocket-book, and all that giddy crowd that this poor, foolish boy thought were his friends desert him in a day.

How many times I have had young men come to me to help them get employment. They tell me of their better days, of how they had come to town with so much money, and with such a good start, and I have said to them: "Why don't you go to your friends? Surely you must have some acquaintances and friends that will stand by you in this emergency." And then I have seen the blush rise in the cheek, and the sullen look of shame come in the eye, as the young fellow says, "I had friends while I had money; but since my money is all gone my friends are gone, too." Ah, that's the way the devil treats a man every time.

Well, this young fellow that Christ tells us about thought he would make the best of it and try to get something to do to earn his living. He had tried all his friends, and not one would help him. Then he went to a hog-raiser and asked if he had any work for him, and he said: "Yes, I need another hog-feeder. Go and feed my swine." And this young fellow that came into this far country with fine clothes, flashing with jewels, and who lived for a time with fast horses and gay friends and rich banquets, goes out into the swine-field in his rags to work for wages so poor that he can not keep himself from being hungry, and "would fain have filled his belly with the husks that the swine did eat, and no man gave unto him." While he watches the swine eat he envies them. Then there comes a blessed thought into his mind; it startles him, and he wonders he had not thought of it before. This is the thought that so arouses him: How is it that in my father's house there is bread enough and to spare, and I perish with hunger? I will rise and go to my father, and say unto him, Father, I have sinned against heaven and before thee, and am no more worthy to be called thy son: make me as one of thy hired servants.

Now the blessed thing about this story is that he did not, like Pharaoh, or Balaam, or Judas, let his good thoughts and desires expend their force in a day-dream and end in wallowing still deeper among the swine. He at once began to put his new light into conduct. He dropped his swineherd staff and started for the highway. If you had passed along that road that night, you would have seen a sign up on the side of the barn, "Another boy wanted to feed hogs." The young man who had turned his face toward home kept steadily toward it. Possibly he had to beg his way from door to door, but he was getting nearer home every day, every hour; every hill he climbed was one less barrier between him and his father's house, where there was plenty. At last he comes in sight of the old home. I can see the tears run down his cheek as he beholds again all the beautiful sights of his childhood, and recalls many a boyish reminiscence of the happy days of his youth. Then possibly a fear rises up in his heart, and he says to himself: "I wonder if father is alive yet? It would be awful to come back and find that I can never see him again, and tell him how sorry I am. And my poor mother! I was always her pet. In my wildest days I used every once in a while to see her face, and the sorrow in it when she bade me good-by." And just then, while he is wondering, and fearful, and his heart is as sore as his feet, he sees somebody coming out from the house, and in a moment he sees that whoever it is he is running; and all at once he shouts: "Why, it's father! It's father himself!" And the sight of his father running to him, and, as he gets closer, the kindness in his face, put new nerve into his own tired legs, and the boy runs too. The running father and the running son soon meet. The father throws his arms around his neck and covers the boy's face with kisses, and then the son begins to try to make the set speech that he had been fixing up all the way home. He had rehearsed it over to himself a thousand times, and he begins, "Father, I have sinned against heaven and in thy sight, and am no more worthy to be called thy son," and he was going to say, "make me as one of thy hired servants." But he never got that far. The father kissed him so and hugged him so that he never got it out. Then the father bursts out in a speech that was all spontaneous, springing right out of his big heart: "Bring forth quickly the best robe, and put it on him; and put a ring on his hand, and shoes on his feet: and bring the fatted calf, and kill it, and let us eat, and make merry: for this my son was dead, and is alive again; he was lost, and is found." And they began to be merry. That poor fellow went away from home and squandered everything he had trying to have a good time, but finds out at last that the only really good place to have a good time is at home.

This is the example I would have you follow. Put your good desires into steps that lead home. Every one of you who is a wanderer away from God may come back and find that, instead of being overdrawn, this story of the prodigal but faintly portrays the happy welcome which God will give you if you obey his invitation and, confessing your sins, come back again to your Father's house. Don't delay! Every day's delay makes it harder. Come now!

IX.

THE DIVINE ANOINTING.

And ye have an anointing from the Holy One, and ye know all things.—*1 John* ii. 20 (*Revised Version*).

JOHN is a great hand to encourage people. His big heart, full and brimming over with the joy of Christian fellowship, evermore rejoicing in the presence of God, makes him an inspiring writer concerning the privileges of the Christian life. He is referring here to the divine anointing which may come to every sincere disciple of Jesus. It is not some great blessing which belongs to an elect few, but one which is the privilege of every child of God. This word "unction" or "anointing" comes from the practise of consecrating priests and kings by the pouring on of holy oil, and its teaching is that the Christian is consecrated to the Christ life, a royal, kingly life, a priestly life in its divine influence, by being endowed with the presence of God's Spirit, who abides with those who surrender their lives completely to do the will of Christ. Such lives are joyous and noble and bear testimony everywhere to the power of God's grace to transform and beautify the human soul.

I think there are many Christians who hold

themselves back from the complete surrender of their lives to Christ, from a self-abandonment to God, through false ideas of what this life of the Spirit means. They have seen some fanatical presentation of Christian holiness, one that lacked intelligence and coherence, and so they hesitate to yield completely the heart and life to be possessed and mastered by the Spirit of God. Surely that is a very unwise thing for us to do. We belong to God; we shall never be as good men and women as we ought to be until God rules in every avenue of our heart. No part of our nature can be held back from divine control without being by that act marred and dwarfed.

We need to distinguish between a life positively good and one that is negatively faultless. While we live in these human bodies and are subjected to the conditions of life in this world, none of us will live faultless lives; but we may so yield our purposes and motives and the very sources of conduct to the control of Jesus Christ that our lives will be blameless in his sight. There is a great difference between that which is faultless and that which is blameless. It is possible for a deed to have many faults and yet not only be blameless, but praiseworthy in the highest degree. Some poet pictures a mother making this distinction while mending the clothes of her little children. The mother says:

> "I was sitting alone in the twilight,
> With spirit troubled and vexed,

With thoughts that were morbid and gloomy,
   And faith that was sadly perplexed.

"Some homely work I was doing
   For the child of my love and care;
Some stitches half wearily setting
   In the endless need of repair.

"But my thoughts were about the building,
   The work some day to be tried,
And that only the gold and the silver
   And the precious stones should abide.

"And remembering my own poor efforts,
   The wretched work I had done,
And even when trying most truly,
   The meager success I had won:

"'It is nothing but wood, hay, and stubble,'
   I said; 'it will all be burned;
This useless fruit of the talents
   One day to be returned;

"'And I have so longed to serve Him,
   And sometimes I know I have tried;
But I'm sure when He sees such building,
   He will never let it abide.'

"Just then, as I turned the garment,
   That no rent should be left behind,
Mine eye caught an odd little bungle
   Of mendings and patchwork combined.

"My heart grew suddenly tender,
   And something blinded my eyes
With one of those sweet inspirations
   That sometimes make us so wise.

"Dear child! she wanted to help me,
  I knew 'twas the best she could do;
But oh! what a botch she had made of it,
  The gray mismatching the blue!

"And yet, can you understand it?
  With a tender smile and a tear,
And a half-compassionate yearning,
  I felt her grow more dear.

"Then a sweet voice broke the silence,
  And the dear Lord said to me,
'Art thou tenderer for thy little child
  Than I am tender for thee?'

"Then straightway I knew His meaning,
  So full of compassion and love;
And my faith came back to its refuge
  Like the glad returning dove.

"So, I thought, when the Master Builder
  Comes down this temple to view,
To see what rents must be mended,
  And what must be builded anew;

"Perhaps as He looks o'er the building
  He will bring my work to the light;
And seeing the marring and bungling,
  And how far it is all from right,

"He will feel as I felt for my darling,
  And will say as I said for her,
'Dear child! she wanted to help Me,
  And love for Me was the spur;

"'And for the great love that is in it
  The work shall seem perfect as Mine';

And, because it was willing service,
   He will crown it with plaudit divine.

"And there in the deepening twilight,
   I seemed to be clasping a hand,
And to feel a great love constraining,
   Far stronger than any command.

"Then I knew by the thrill of sweetness,
   'Twas the Hand of the Blessed One
Which should tenderly guide and hold me,
   Till all the labor is done.

"So my thoughts are nevermore gloomy,
   My faith is no longer dim;
But my heart is strong and restful,
   And mine eyes are unto Him."

It is the happy privilege of the Christian to live in consciousness of the presence of God's Spirit in his heart. God's Spirit will never leave us except through our sins. If we are not conscious of his presence with us and feel that the Comforter has been withdrawn, we may be sure that the fault is our own. When you turn the faucet in your kitchen, the water pours out and fills your empty bucket; that is, it will so long as your pipes are connected with the water main and the greater reservoir behind it. But when that connection has been broken the faucet only mocks you. When I came home from vacation last summer and opened up the parsonage, I could not get a drop of water anywhere in the house. I went down in the cellar and turned it on where we usually do, but no water came. Then I telephoned for a plumber, and he went into the cellar and examined the pipes, and said the water ought to come, but that the fault must be out in the street, and that the city authorities for some reason must have turned the water off. Then I telephoned to the Water Works office and found that the water rent had not been paid, and so the water had been turned off while we were away. I paid the water-rate, and then an employee came and turned the water on in the street, and the water poured forth at our desire all over the house. But you see the law had to be made good first. So long as I was a sinner against the water law, I had no connection with the great reservoir and its abundance. Are there any here this morning whose sins have severed their connection with the reservoir of the Water of Life? If so, the remedy is as simple in your case as it was in mine. Repent of your sin, and, through faith in Jesus Christ, seek forgiveness for it, and you shall come into that relation to God that he shall pour on you all spiritual blessing.

This is a wonderful declaration in the last sentence of our text, "Ye know all things." That means all things that are necessary to spiritual life. The soul that surrenders itself to Christ is spiritually taught. It is a kind of training that can not come in any other way. It can not be bought for gold, it can not be had by any sort of self-discipline; it must come by surrender to Christ, through personal communion with the Savior and the Holy Spirit.

The result of this anointing and spiritual insight is that whoever receives it becomes spiritually courageous. See what a change it made in Peter. Impulsive and bold as he was about ordinary matters, he was a great coward when it came to talking about his friendship with Christ. The night that Jesus was betrayed Peter turned white and denied his Lord in the presence of a servant-maid. There are Christians now who have the same cowardice when it comes to talking about their relation to Christ. They are bold enough in talking about business, or politics, or social affairs; but when the friends of Jesus come together they say that they are too timid and afraid to speak. If you will surrender your whole heart and life to Christ and receive the full anointing of the Holy Spirit, it will give you courage as it did Peter. Peter never was troubled that way after the day of Pentecost. People marked the boldness of Peter and the other disciples. Their fear of God took away their fear of men. Their love for Christ and their devotion to him were so strong that everything else seemed small and insignificant and had no power to hold them back from bold testimony for Christ.

Another effect is that it fills the heart with love and sympathy for sinners. I do believe we need that more than anything else to make us the successful workers we ought to be in seeking after the unconverted and in winning them to Christ. We need to come into such fellowship with Christ, to be so possessed and controlled by his spirit, that love will master every motive and purpose of our being. We ought not only to commit to memory, but to engrave on our hearts, Paul's wonderful thirteenth chapter in his first letter to the Corinthians: "If I speak with the tongues of men and of angels, but have not love, I am become sounding brass, or a clanging cymbal. And if I have the gift of prophecy, and know all mysteries and all knowledge; and if I have all faith, so as to remove mountains, but have not love, I am nothing. And if I bestow all my goods to feed the poor, and if I give my body to be burned, but have not love, it profiteth me nothing. Love suffereth long, and is kind; love envieth not; love vaunteth not itself, is not puffed up, doth not behave itself unseemly, seeketh not its own, is not provoked, taketh not account of evil; rejoiceth not in unrighteousness, but rejoiceth with the truth; beareth all things, believeth all things, hopeth all things, endureth all things. Love never faileth: but whether there be prophecies, they shall be done away; whether there be tongues, they shall cease; whether there be knowledge, it shall be done away. . . . But now abideth faith, hope, love, these three; and the greatest of these is love. Follow after love." May God give us that divine anointing that shall fill our hearts with love toward our fellow men so that we shall endure all things in order to win them to our Christ!

If we are thus anointed by the Spirit of God, there will be a charm about us that will make itself felt through all prejudice and overcome all objections. In the old slavery days the owner of a plantation, on buying a slave, said to the person of whom he was purchasing him, "Tell me honestly what are his faults?" Said the seller, "He has no faults that I am aware of but one: that one fault is, he will pray." "Ah!" said the purchaser, "I don't like that; but I know something that will cure him of it pretty soon." So the next night Cuffey was surprised by his master in the plantation while in earnest prayer, praying for his new master, and his master's wife and family. The man stood and listened, but said nothing at the time; but the next morning he called Cuffey, and said: "I do not want to quarrel with you, my man, but I'll have no praying on my premises; so you just drop it." "Massa," said he, "me canna leave off praying; me must pray." "I'll teach you to pray, if you are going to keep on at it." "Massa, me must keep on." "Well, then, I'll give you five-and-twenty lashes a day till you leave off." "Massa, if you give me fifty I must pray." "If that's the way you are saucy to your master, you shall have it at once." So, tying him up, he gave him five-and-twenty lashes, and asked him if he would pray again. "Yes, massa, me must pray always; canna

THE DIVINE ANOINTING. 85

leave off." The master looked astonished; he could not understand how a poor fellow could keep on praying when it seemed to do no good, but only brought persecution on him. He told his wife about it. His wife said: "Why can't you let the poor man pray? He does his work very well; you and I do not care about praying, but there's no harm in letting him pray if he gets on with his work." "But I don't like it," said the master; "he almost frightened me to death. You should see how he looked at me." "Was he angry?" "No, I should not have minded that; but after I had beaten him he looked at me with tears in his eyes as if he pitied me more than himself." That night the master could not sleep; he tossed to and fro on his bed; his sins were brought to his remembrance; the face of the old black man whom he had beaten for praying stared him in the face, and those tearful, loving eyes haunted him. Rising in his bed, he said, "Wife, will you pray for me?" "I never prayed in my life," said she; "I can not pray for you." "I am lost," he said, "if somebody does not pray for me; I can not pray for myself." "I don't know any one on the estate that knows how to pray except Cuffey," said his wife. The bell was rung and Cuffey was brought in. Taking hold of his black servant's hand, the master said, "Cuffey, can you pray for your master?" "Massa," said he, "me been praying for you eber since you flogged me, and me means to pray always for you." Down went Cuffey on his knees and poured out his soul in pleadings and tears until both husband and wife were converted. Neither anger nor prejudice nor infidelity could stand out against the spiritual power, the marvelous spiritual charm, that was in that old black man's soul.

Dear friends, that is what we need, and what we must have, if we are to do the work of God. Are you willing to seek it? Are you willing to receive it? Are you willing to surrender all to Christ? It can not come from any half-hearted surrender; it must be a complete surrender of the soul to God. But why should we hold back? "Nothing but sin have we to give," but everything that is beautiful and lovely and glorious shall we receive in return.

Great destiny hangs on our decision. There are within our reach scores of men and women, yes, hundreds of them, who can only be won by us when we are at white heat of devotion and clothed upon by the Spirit of God. In the condition we are in now we will not win them, but God can equip us so that they will yield to our persuasion and our influence. From many a town, and many a country place, young men and young women have flocked to this city, and are here in the midst of its temptations, running the fearful gantlet of sin on every side. They are being wounded and hurt and many are being destroyed. No lukewarm Christianity will win them; no mere formal expression of our interest in them, or our faith in Christ, will attract their attention. But if the Holy Spirit shall dwell in us, as he did in Paul when he felt that he would rather be accursed than fail to save the people to whom he preached, or as he did in Stephen when his face shone like an angel in the presence of the men who had sworn away his life by perjured testimony, or as he inspired Peter and the hundred and twenty men and women who were with him on the day of Pentecost until three thousand were saved in one day,—if that Spirit be in us then we shall win like victories. We shall be able to attract men's attention on their downward rush toward hell. We shall be able to show them the beauty of Christ. We shall be able to reveal to them the loveliness of Christian character. In the light of the holy earnestness that will clothe our faces and our conversation, and inspire our deeds, a worldly and a sensual life will seem dull and mean to them, and they will long to know the Christ, fellowship with whom has made such a transformation in us. May God bestow on us the holy anointing!

X.

A PASSING LUST BUT AN ABIDING SOUL.

And the world passeth away, and the lust thereof; but he that doeth the will of God abideth for ever.—*1 John* ii. 17.

EVERYTHING that belongs only to this world is very changeable and uncertain, and is rapidly passing away. Nothing is more changeable than the conditions of human life. A baby soon changes into a child, the child into a youth, the youth into the man or woman. The strength of middle life soon passes, and old age draws on apace. If I were to call upon these white-haired men and women to bear testimony, they would tell you that the most astonishing things they have known in life, even when it has stretched through fourscore years and more, have been its brevity and its changeableness. Life is like the current of a stream that swings about the point of land that cuts athwart its tide. It is ever passing—passing away to come back no more. And we are assured in our text that the world itself will soon pass away, and that if that were not so it would be all the same to us, for our passion for it would soon be gone anyway.

The lust for worldly things is a very transient passion. A man soon loses his appetite and zest for all worldly pleasures. Take the pleasures of the athletic field, or of the chase, or all pleasures that have to do simply with physical exercise, the enjoyment of physical being—they are very transient. The passing years soon take the suppleness out of the joints, the spring out of nerve and muscle, the restless heat out of the blood; and the armchair and the quiet of the fireside appeal more strongly than the vigorous life that once gave such enjoyment. Every such life is an illustration of the truth of the text that the lust of the world soon passeth away.

It is so with all worldly things. It is as true of money-making and money-spending as of anything else. One of the richest men in New York was met on the street one day and congratulated by a friend on occupying the most enviable position in the world. For, said his friend, "you have everything that heart can wish." But the rich man said: "I am one of the most miserable men in the world. I have a great mansion, but I can not enjoy it. I must spend my days in trying to keep from losing what I have got. I can order the best food in the world, but my health is so poor that I can scarcely eat anything that I want. I am so beset by schemers and tricksters and beggars that I scarcely ever breathe in peace without suspicion that somebody is trying to rob me. I have fast horses, and my nerves are in such a state that I am afraid to drive behind them. I can not sleep at night. I was just thinking, when

I met you and you congratulated me, that I was the most miserable man in the city." He was an illustration of the truth of this text, that the lust of this world passeth away.

There is nothing permanent except that which is spiritual. What folly, then, to spend all the time on the body and on this earthly life, to the exclusion of the development of those noble powers of the soul that shall live forever! Mr. Ingersoll, in his printed reply to me the other day, sneers at Jesus Christ, who, he says, advised men to spend their time in this world in preparing for the next world. Well, why not? Would not Mr. Ingersoll have a baby spend its time getting strength and exercise and skill to fit it for the experiences of boyhood and girlhood? Would he not advise the boy and girl to spend their time in school, developing body and mind for the duties of manhood and womanhood? And if man is an immortal being, created for an endless life in high and lofty fellowships, what better thing can he do during the years of manhood than so to use his business ability that he shall develop the great qualities of honesty and truth; that a woman shall so use her social gifts that she shall develop the great qualities of integrity and love; that both man and woman shall so deal with this world that it shall be to them a scaffolding in which there is growing up a strong and noble character, that after a while, when the scaffolding of earth is taken down, the strong and beautiful and chastened soul shall be ready for its immortal career? Our observation shows us that this life is infinitely more valuable to the man who uses it as a school-room, as a place of discipline for a still nobler life beyond, than it is to him who uses it as a loafing-room or a place of revel.

In the midst of these passing conditions of worldly life Christ comes and offers us a life that shall abide forever. He offers us pleasures that do not pass away. He offers us the treasure of a good conscience; and what a precious thing that is! To be able to look all men in the face, with the consciousness that, in so far as you know, you are seeking, by God's help, to do what is right toward God and man. To lie down and sleep at night with the sweet assurance that you are at peace with God; that through Jesus Christ your sins are all forgiven, and that there is no condemnation against you. A good conscience you may carry with you always; it will be as priceless a treasure when you are eighty as it was when you were twenty. It will shine forth brighter than diamonds in a dying hour, and it will be more brilliant than the sun at the judgment seat. It is one of the treasures that will never pass away.

Fellowship with Christian friends and glad anticipation of meeting with loved ones whom we "have loved long since and lost awhile" is also a treasure which does not pass away with the years. As I have grown older I have watched with greatest interest to note what were the chief interests to old people who are Christians, and I have observed with great comfort that their joy in Christian society, their happiness in listening to Christian testimony, their gladness in witnessing the conversion of sinners, and their hope in the communion with loved ones in the world to come, are the supreme enjoyments of Christian souls as they get nearer to the bounds of this world's life. These are pleasures that neither time nor fortune nor any of the changing fashions of the world can alter for a moment, and they are most convincing proof that John's word is true, that "He that doeth the will of God abideth forever."

Now Christ comes, not asking us to give up this present life, not requiring that we shall drape it with gloom, but that we shall make it the more joyous and precious by bringing into it this element of permanency, so that all that we do in this world shall make us more fit for the glory of our immortal career. How foolish is the man who throws away his chance for eternal life in heaven in order that he may only mar and spoil the life which now is! We can not have the joys of fellowship with Christ in heaven if we are ashamed of him here. Jesus says: "Whosoever shall be ashamed of me and of my words in this adulterous and sinful generation, the Son of man also shall be ashamed of him, when he cometh in the glory of his Father with the holy angels."

I have seen the story of an English soldier who lay on his bed in an infirmary of the barracks. He had received a slight injury and was unable to perform his customary duties. Tho his ailment was not a dangerous one, it was serious enough to keep him to his bed. Time hung heavily on his hands. One day one of his comrades came in and sat down to chat with him. The sick man remarked: "Look here, I am desperately tired of lying here doing nothing. I wish you would go down to the library and find some good novel or some book of that kind and bring it up for me to read." Now both the sick man and his friend were wicked men, who had no thought of goodness. The other replied, "Oh! yes, I will do that for you." He went away to the library, and came back presently with a book in his hand, and putting it on the bed, with a very pious and sanctimonious look, he said, "My good brother, I have brought you a very pious and instructive treatise which I have no doubt will be very profitable to you; it is James's 'Anxious Inquirer.'" On making this remark he burst out into a laugh and left the room. The first impulse of the sick man was to fling the book after him; but he reflected that it was better than nothing, and that if he threw it he would not be able to get it again unless he left his bed, which he was unable to do. After the other was gone he had a curiosity to see what the book was like. He opened it and read the first few chapters; and, strange to say, he was wonderfully interested; no novel ever interested him more than that book. But he was terribly afraid lest any one should catch him reading it. If he heard any one on the staircase, or saw a person pass the door, the book was under his pillow in a moment. He went on reading; and the more he read, the more miserable he became. As he lay there in his bed it seemed as if all his past life rose up before him—its guilt, debauchery, and the wretched souls that he had helped to destroy. Day after day his convictions deepened, until he made up his mind that he could go on with his sinful life no longer. He began to pray. He promised God that as soon as he left the infirmary he would join the little band of Christian men who were accustomed to meet in a room a few hundred yards from the barracks to read the Bible together. That evening came, and he set forth from the barracks. As he drew near the place he noticed that right across from him was the great gin-palace where he had been in the habit of spending his evenings. He went on until he stood in the middle between the two places. He was between two opposing influences. There arose within his mind the thought: "Now, then, you are not going to turn your back on all your old life. Look at that gin-palace; you have had many pleasant times there; now if you go down to those saints, just think what a life you will lead in the regiment; the life of a dog would be nothing to it. You can not stand that." He stood transfixed for a few minutes, and could not move from the spot. At last his courage began to give way, and he walked slowly toward the gin-palace. He reached the door; he laid his hand on the door-handle, and was just going to enter, when suddenly it seemed as if a voice of thunder spoke to him. There was no outward sound, but that terrible voice came rolling through his inmost soul like the voice of doom, and the words it uttered were: "Whosoever shall be ashamed of me and of my words in this adulterous and sinful generation, of him also shall the Son of man be ashamed when he cometh in the glory of his Father, with the holy angels." He let the door-handle drop as if it were red-hot. He turned from the threshold of the gin-palace and faced toward the door of the little room where those good men were sitting reading the Word of God. Once again he was about to open the door, when the thought came to his mind: "How queer they will all look at you! There is not a man in the regiment they would be more surprised to see than you. What will you say? How silly you will feel! How foolish you will look!" And as these thoughts rose up in his mind, again he found himself standing stock still, and the tempter said to him: "Go home, go home; do not make a fool of yourself." As he stood hesitating, for the second time there came thundering through his soul that tremendous voice of power, "Whosoever shall be ashamed of me and of my words, of him shall the Son of man be ashamed;" and as the words rang in his ears he gave the door a push and sprang into the room. If a bomb-shell had dropped into their midst, these Christians could not have looked more surprised than they did. But one of them had presence of mind enough to greet him in a friendly sort of way, and said, "Well, my dear fellow, have you come to read the Bible with us?" "Yes," he said, "I have come because I want to turn over a new leaf." "Thank God! You are the man we want." He found he was among true friends and brothers. Every one had a kind word and a warm welcome for him. They stopped the Bible-reading, and all knelt down and prayed with him; but still he did not find peace; his heart was filled with doubt and fear; he crawled back to the barracks as miserable as he could be. When he entered the barrack-room, it was like going from the porch of heaven to the gate of hell. One man was singing an obscene song; another was telling a filthy tale; another was swearing and blaspheming at the top of his voice; all was vile, and for the first time in his life he was horrified by it. It was probably no worse than usual, but he had never noticed it before. Now the whole thing was revolting to him. He crept to his bedside and sat there, lost in a reverie of conflicting emotions. He was wondering what he should do next; and at last he thought he would get into bed and have a quiet time of meditation and prayer, turning over in his mind all that he had heard from the men at the prayer-meeting. He undressed himself and was on the point of stepping into bed. For the third time that tremendous voice came thundering through his soul, "Whosoever shall be ashamed of me and of my words, of him shall the Son of man be ashamed." He dropped on his knees as if he had been shot, and cried aloud, "Great God, have mercy upon me, a sinner!" Well, if those Christian men had been electrified when they saw him staggering into their midst, these reckless soldiers in the barrack-room were vastly more astonished. They stood there gaping in amazement; they did not say a word. They knew what a wicked life he had led, and there they stood dumb and astonished. By and by one stole off to his bed, and another, and another, and they left him alone. They did not say a rough word to him; they were too much surprised. They knew it was the power of God. The battle was won now; all the barriers of pride and shame were swept away, and light and joy and peace burst upon his soul.

I doubt not that I am now speaking to some who need just this heart-searching message. You are giving all your time and thought to the present life, indifferent to the life of the soul, which is infinitely more important. Whatever you may say with your lips, the testimony of your life is a rejection of Christ and all his tender invitations. Your life says that you are ashamed of him and of his words. And if you were to die as you are to-night you would compel him to be ashamed of you at the great Judgment. May God give you wisdom to turn now to Christ and confess him here, that he may not be ashamed of you hereafter!

XI.

MEETING CHRIST WITHOUT SHAME.

Abide in him; that, if he shall be manifested, we may have boldness, and not be ashamed before him at his coming. —*1 John* ii. 28.

To abide in Christ is to live in his spirit, to do the things that are pleasing to him. If we live in that spirit here, we shall meet Christ without shame. There is no more solemn thought than that we must give an account for our deeds, and that the day is swiftly coming when we must meet Christ and give an account for our treatment of him. Pilate's old question, "What shall I do with this Jesus that is called Christ?" is a question with which every one of us has to deal. If we reject him now, he will reject us in the great Day of Account; if we are indifferent to him, we bar out his interference in our behalf in the Day of Judgment. But if we confess him now, he will confess us in the great Assize. If we give him our hearts and abide in him, living in his spirit, we shall meet him not with shame, but with joy and unspeakable delight.

There ought to be a word here for us as Christians. Are we so working for Christ, so spreading abroad the good news of his salvation, so giving up our own luxury and desires that are selfish, in order to win souls to him, that when we meet him we shall be glad to show him what we have done? It is a sad thing to go empty-handed into eternity to meet the Lord.

Some years ago a man lay dying. He had lived a Christian life, and his conduct had been so irreproachable that he was greatly esteemed by all who knew him. But he had not given great attention to persuading others to seek Christ. When he came to die, his sons stood round his bed, hanging upon their father's lips and prepared to treasure the last words which he should speak to them in this life. One of his sons asked, "Father, are you not afraid to die?" There was a pause, as if the dying man turned his mental gaze in upon himself, and then slowly he replied: "No, no! I am not afraid to die, but," and he lifted his wasted hand, "I am almost ashamed to die when I look back on my wasted years that might have been spent in far more active service for my Lord." Let no Christian here be putting thorns in his dying pillow by the lethargy of his Christian life. Let us work with all our hearts while the day lasts, so that we shall be able to bring our sheaves to the Master not with shame but with rejoicing.

And you that are not Christians, is it not true that you are doing with comparative indifference many things that are wrong, that you would hesitate to do if you kept the thought before you that you must face them all before the judgment seat of Christ at the last? I think some people are deluded into thinking that their sins are somehow lost by being hidden away by the passing years. But sin never gets forgiven that way. In God's universe there is no dusty garret where you can hide sins.

An old man tells the story of how, when he was a boy, he went into his father's orchard, and there in his rough play he broke a little tree of a precious variety which his father valued very much. But rapidly putting it together again, he was able to conceal the fact, for the disunited parts of the tree fitted back close together, and the tree stood as before. Half a century passed by, and the lad, now grown into a gray-haired man, went into that orchard after a storm had blown across it in the night, and he found the tree had been torn in two —it had snapped precisely in the place where he had broken it when it was but a sapling. So we often see men who go down in their character with a crash, and, if you hunt into it, you find that it is a place where they sinned when they were boys. The only way to assure yourself that your sin will not bring you to shame and disgrace is to bring your sin to shame now by confessing it and finding forigveness in Christ's mercy. Mr. Spurgeon says that when the trumpet of resurrection sounds there will be a resurrection of characters as well as of men. The man who has been foully slandered will rejoice in the light that reflects his purity. But the man whose latent vices have been skilfully veneered will be brought to the light, too; his acts and motives will be alike exposed. As he himself sees the resurrection of his crimes, with what horror will he face that Day of Judgment! "Ah! ah!" says he; "where am I? I had forgotten these things. These are the sins of my childhood, the sins of my youth, the sins of my young manhood. I thought they were dead and buried, but they start from their tombs. My memory has been quickened. How my brain reels as I think of them all! But there they are, and, like so many wolves around me, they seem all thirsting for my destruction." O my friends, let us not be self-deceived! There is no escaping sin by burying it. Let God bury it. He has promised that if we will repent of our sins and forsake them he will not only forgive them, but he will drown them in the depths of the sea, where they shall never trouble us again. There is only One that is strong enough to slay these wolf-like sins, and that is Jesus Christ, our Savior. Let him slay your sins now, and you will meet him without shame after a while.

Many of you have others besides your Savior who have gone on before you into the heavenly world and have begged you to meet them there. Some of you have given sacred promises of that sort, promises which can never be redeemed except

MEETING CHRIST WITHOUT SHAME. 103

by forsaking your sins and finding pardon in Jesus' name. How are you going to meet these dear ones without shame? You know the only way you can do so is by turning to Christ for salvation. Dr. Aitkin tells of a mother whom he knew, who, when she came to die, called her children around her. As they approached her bed, one by one, she stretched out her hand and took theirs in hers, and very solemnly, for she was on the brink of eternity, said to them, "I charge you before God, meet me at God's right hand." When it came to the turn of her eldest son, she was greatly moved, for up to that time he had shown no disposition to become a Christian. She grasped his hand in hers, and said, with tears in her eyes: "My boy, ere I die, I want you to make me a promise; I want you to solemnly promise me that you will seek the salvation of your soul." He hesitated, and stood silent for a few moments, hanging his head. When he lifted up his eyes, he met his mother's gaze. That deep, tender, earnest gaze seemed to plead with his inmost heart. "I charge you," she said, "meet me at God's right hand." "Mother," he said, "I will; I will." Her face brightened up; a heavenly smile stole over her features; she lifted up her hands, and said, "Thank God, I am ready to go now."

Well, she died. The boy remembered his promise. He began to read his Bible, and great conviction of sin came upon him. He became very wretched. Weeks passed by, and tho he could not shake the subject from his mind, he found no peace. He was sitting in his room one day with this weight of conscious guilt upon his soul, when suddenly he jumped up and said, "I really can not stand this any longer." He grasped his hat and dashed out, with the determination to drown his sorrows in drink at the nearest saloon. Just as he stood at the door and was stretching out his hand to open it, it seemed to him as tho his mother stood before him. There was the same look upon her countenance that it wore when she took leave of him on her dying bed, and he seemed to see those tears glistening in her eyes. It was no vision, but it was all so powerfully brought before his imagination that it was like a vision, and he seemed to hear her saying, "My son, your promise!" He turned and fled from the wicked place as if he were pursued. He dashed into his own room. "O God," he cried, "thou hast saved me by my mother's prayer; thou hast saved me from the depths of hell!" And there in his own room he cast himself in utter weariness and helplessness at Jesus' feet, and the pardoning love of Christ reached his heart. And then he knew with great joy that he could meet his mother at the right hand of God in peace and not be ashamed.

There is nothing that this world can give you that can pay you for the loss of peace with God and a hope in Jesus Christ that will make it possible for you to meet death and eternity without shame. Everything that promises permanent peace by merely worldly resources is a delusion and a snare. There is what is called a "will-o'-the-wisp." It is brought about by natural causes. A dim light is sometimes seen hovering over marshy places, like the pale flame at the end of a burning stick when it separates itself for a moment from the stick and trembles in the air before it goes out. Educated people know that this light is produced by natural causes, and is found only in places where decayed wood or animal matter is in the water; but it has always been an object of terror to the ignorant. Weird stories used to be told regarding it; how men lost in the darkness of the night saw this lambent light, which looked like a candle carried by some unseen person who was going home; and how, allured by the hope of finding shelter and guidance, they turned aside to follow it, when, as they came nearer, it moved on farther and farther, until at last it led its unhappy victims to a deep bog into which they stumbled and were drowned. How many men and women there are to-day who are being lured by sin's will-o'-the-wisp into destruction! The evil one promises abiding pleasure and comfort in sin; but such promises are never kept. The poor sinner is led on and on, until he is drowned in wicked habits, chained by his own iniquities, and stands ashamed and confused in the presence of the Savior who offered to guide him in the path of light and salvation.

When the great emergency of life comes and you must go forth to meet the future, there is not wealth enough in the universe to buy from you, if you have it, a good conscience and a peaceful heart that will enable you to meet Christ and your friends in joy and gladness. A ship coming home from Australia to England caught fire. The passengers and crew took to two boats, one a large and the other a small one. Into the smaller boat had been cast in the confusion and the hurry of the moment several cases containing solid gold to the value of a great many thousands of dollars. In the large boat there was a considerable quantity of provisions; in the smaller boat only a very slender supply, but this large amount of gold. The men pulled away from the burning ship; there was a stiff breeze rising, and they knew that in all probability they should not see each other when the day dawned; so before they separated they began to overhaul their provisions. The men on board the smaller boat found that they only had a meager supply. A man who was there says that he can never forget the moment when three or four stalwart sailors lifted up a huge case of gold, held it before the eyes of the men in the other boat, and shouted across the water, "Ten thousand pounds for one cask of bacon!" That was a big price, but the men would not look at it. That one cask of bacon was worth to them more than all the gold in the world. On it their very life might depend: they could feed life on the bacon, but they could not on the gold.

Dear friends, this life is swiftly passing. This short school-day of human life will soon be over, and in that great hour when you are going out into eternity all the pleasures of the world and all the gold there is in it will seem as nothing compared to a pure heart, a good conscience, friendship with Jesus Christ, so that you may meet him without shame. You may have them all without money and without price. Come to Christ and live!

XII.

THE MANNER OF GOD'S LOVE.

Behold what manner of love the Father hath bestowed upon us, that we should be called the children of God: and such we are.—*1 John* iii. 1 (*Revised Version*).

SURELY there can be no study more suggestive or more comforting to us than to reflect upon the manner of God's love as expressed in his Word and in his dealing with us. There is something magnificent and sublime in the way Almighty God, the Creator and Ruler of the universe, bowing himself to our need, makes his love and mercy and sympathy appear greater to us than either his wisdom or his power. We have God presented to us here, as in many other places in the Bible, under the title of Father—not a father who is arbitrary and autocratic, regarding the home as something created for him, but as the true, the ideal father, who is the servant of the home, who day by day gives his broad shoulders to toil or his judgment to devise for the benefit of every boy and girl in the home; who puts aside his own interests and denies himself that the least as well as the greatest in the home may be comforted and nourished.

If you will glance through both the Old and the

New Scriptures, surely nothing will be more impressive than the gracious names by which God reveals to us the manner of his love. And you will notice that in every case they represent God as one using his strength and his wisdom in humble and sympathetic service in behalf of the children of his love. Take the picture that David gives us in the twenty-third Psalm, "The Lord is my shepherd." The shepherd gives all his thought and all his care, day and night, to the sheep. He is ever within reach to defend them if necessary from their enemies, and to guide them into green pastures and beside the still waters, where they may slake their thirst and be fed. If the shadows fall about them on the way home at night, it is his cheering voice and his rod and his staff that are their comfort. If one is lost and left behind, he is the one that goes back through the night, leaving the ninety and nine safe in the fold, and searches after the lost till he finds it. And when he finds it, worn-out and frightened, and it may be wounded, he puts it on his shoulder and carries it home rejoicing. Could there be anything more tender than the manner of Good's love suggested in that picture?

I think many people stay away from the service of God because they have altogether a wrong idea about God. Many people think about God as a great czar, a sort of exaggerated sultan, or emperor, who sits on the throne of the universe and is surrounded by the adulations of millions in his place of inaccessible glory. There could not be a more false idea of God than that, and yet I think it is quite a popular idea. Surely it is not the idea of God as presented in the Bible. The Bible shows us a God who is the Father of his creatures; who is the Shepherd that lovingly cares not only for man, but for everything that he has made. He is so watchful that not even a sparrow falls to the ground without his notice. The flowers spring forth under his smile, and he gives to the meadow lilies a beauty more splendid than a king can command. Christ presents this same idea of God. He came not to be ministered unto, but to minister. He was the greatest servant that this world has ever seen. A blind beggar could stop him anywhere, and the most hopeless leper could have his services as readily as a nobleman or a ruler. He was ever ministering to the needs of the weak and the poor. Christ carried his heart on his sleeve, and anybody could have it for the asking. It was but an emblem of his whole life when he girded himself with a towel, and took a basin of water, and went about among the disciples, washing their feet. And in all this we are assured that Christ was showing God to us; he was revealing to us the manner of the Father's love. We know this is true because he says so. In one of those tender conversations which Christ had with his disciples just before his crucifixion, Philip, lonely and heart-sick at the thought of Christ's going away from them, cried out to Jesus, "Oh, show us the Father and it sufficeth us." And Jesus immediately answered: "What! Have I, then, been so long with you, Philip, and yet hast thou not known that he that hath seen me hath seen the Father? How sayest thou, then, Show us the Father?" This picture of God as a father, and this assurance that his love is in the same manner as a father's love, ought to bring God very close to us.

A merchant was opening a barrel of apples, when the big, dust-covered, and necessarily untidy man came back with the empty ash-barrel. He picked up an apple and held it out toward him, saying, "Won't you have an apple?"

The man took it eagerly, saying as he did so: "Thank ye, sir; I have a little feller at home who'll be tickled to death to git it. I most always find something or other in the ash-barrels to carry home to him at night, but it ain't often I git anything equal to this big apple. I tell ye, the little feller's eyes will shine when he sees it."

The merchant could not get the picture out of his mind all day, and thought often of the big, rough-handed man with that apple put away so carefully in his pocket for the "little feller" who was on the lookout for the dust-covered father with the calloused and soiled hands. In how many homes such "little fellers" glorify and make beautiful lives that are compelled to struggle against poverty!

But the human heart is the same thing in a palace as it is in a crowded tenement house. There is a very sweet story told of two little girls and the first Emperor William of Germany. The old king had a daughter whom he loved dearly. But she died when she was quite young, and the king grieved very much. He had a flower called by her name. Two little girls who lived in a village near the palace heard of the king's sorrow and his love for this flower, so they went out into the fields and gathered their arms full of flowers of this kind and carried them to the palace. The way was long, and they came there hot and tired, and the flowers were all dusty and withered. A soldier, who was sentinel at the gate, tried to drive them away, but just then the king came out. They went to him and said that they had brought the flowers because they had heard that he loved them so well. The king very gently took the faded flowers from their arms, and the tears fell from his eyes as he thought of his little daughter. He took the little girls into the palace and had them sit at his own table. They feasted there with all the grand ladies and gentlemen of the court; and they never forgot it to their dying day.

Now if the manner of God's love is like a father's I am sure that we can understand it. It brings us close to him. I pray God that it may bring us so close that we shall all with one accord pour out our gratitude and our love in return at his feet!

If God's love is like a father's, then we can understand Christ's wonderful words about the children: "Suffer little children to come unto me, and forbid them not, for of such is the kingdom of heaven." We ought to bring the children as soon as possible to Christ. There must be children about us, many of them, who by a little thoughtfulness and a little tender solicitude could be brought to Christ these days. I have heard of a good old Scotch elder, who was deeply concerned because his pastor persistently refused to allow children to unite with the church. One day he invited him to his house. After tea, the elder took the pastor out to see his large flock of sheep put into the fold. Taking his stand at the entrance to the sheep-fold, the elder allowed the sheep to enter, but as the little lambs came up he roughly pushed them back with a heavy stick. The pastor became very indignant, and exclaimed: "What are you doing to the lambs? They need the shelter far more than the sheep!" "Just what you are doing to the children of the church," was the prompt reply. The object-lesson did its work. Never again did that pastor attempt to shut out from the fold of the church one of Christ's little ones. Let us look for the children; it only takes a little love to win a child and turn the current of life toward heaven while the stream is small and while there is infinite opportunity for development of a noble and useful character. We were born to be the children of God, and we shall only be dwarfed and blighted specimens of what is possible for us unless we yield ourselves to God's love and permit him to work his will upon our hearts and lives.

There is a very beautiful story told of Ole Bull, the great violinist. Many years ago he was wandering through a frontier forest. In the midst of the forest he came upon a hut occupied by a hermit, who had formerly been a man in public life; but, meeting with some great sorrow and bitter disappointment, he had withdrawn from humanity and built himself this little log cabin in the wilderness. As Ole Bull pushed the door open and stepped in, he looked in wonder upon the white beard of the old hermit. On the wall of the cabin there hung a violin. After a little conversation the great musician pointed to the instrument, and asked, "What is that?" The hermit said, "That is my violin." "Can you play?" "Well, I reckon I can. I got that thirty-five years ago in London." "Would you mind playing a little?" "Certainly not." He took the violin down and began to play as requested. The poor thing wailed "God Save the King" and shrieked "My Country, 'Tis of Thee" and "Home, Sweet Home." As he lowered the violin with a self-satisfied air, Ole Bull asked, timidly, "Do you think I could learn to play?" "Well, I do not know about you; it takes years; but I learned." Ole Bull took the violin and picked his way over the strings with the sweep of the great artist. He then poured his soul into it. He played, as only he could play, "God Save the King," and "My Country, 'Tis of Thee," and the "Carnival of Venice," and "Home, Sweet Home," until the mountains of Norway lifted their rugged summits again before his own imagination, and the streets and faces of his native city appeared again before the mind of the banished politician in the old hermit. They were melted in tears together, such was the power of that little musical instrument of wood and string under the sway of him who was its rightful master.

May God give us the message of this little story! The human heart belongs to God; only he knows how to make its noblest music. The life of Christ was forever illustrating this fact. Jesus was ever taking men and women who had made a failure of everything, and causing them to blossom out into something glorious. That poor demon-possessed man at Gadara—what a miserable thing he had made of life! Devilish passions played upon his heart and awoke only strife and discord and wailing; but under the touch of Jesus, love and gratitude and praise burst forth with their sweetest music. Poor, old, blind Bartimæus—what a failure he was! a miserable, old roadside beggar. But when Christ found him, he awoke a man in him, and I have no doubt that at Pentecost, when three thousand were won to Christ in a single day, Bartimæus with his wondrous testimony was one of the most magnetic and forceful preachers of the one hundred and twenty. And Zacchæus—selfishness and greed had played upon his soul and aroused nothing but what was repulsive. The people hated and despised him, and his own heart was full of unrest and dissatisfaction, but when Jesus begins to play upon his heart what marvelous transformation is there!

My dear friends, Jesus has not lost either his love or his skill; he can take your poor heart, that has been played upon by wicked passions and by evil lusts and unholy desires, from which there have come forth only wails of sorrow or groans of dissatisfaction, and he can make it sing again with music that is full of heavenly peace. Why withhold your heart from him? No one else can deal with it so tenderly as he will. No one else can deal with you so wisely as he. Nothing but good can come from yielding your heart to him.

XIII.

A LOATHSOME RELATIVE AND HOW TO GET RID OF HIM.

He that doeth sin is of the devil; for the devil sinneth from the beginning. To this end was the Son of God manifested, that he might destroy the works of the devil.—*1 John* iii. 8 (*Revised Version*).

WE have here a statement of fact fully as vital and important as our last study, but one that is as fearful and startling as that was soothing and comforting. It is stated, in as plain language as it is possible to use, that when we yield ourselves to sin we become the children of the devil. Our relation to him becomes as intimate as the relation of a child to a parent. We are of him; we spring forth from him, as the branch springs forth from the tree, when we yield our hearts to do his bidding. Christ said to some sinners of his time, "Ye are of your father, the devil." There is nothing pleasant about this statement. It is not a pleasant theme to preach about. I do not choose it because I like to preach about such themes. I choose it because I dare not do otherwise. As God's minister, I must not hesitate to declare unto you the whole counsel of God. There are many curses prophesied for the shepherd that does not to the utmost of his ability do his duty in warning and protecting from the wolves that seek to destroy them those to whom he is sent to minister.

I do not know any other Scripture that more clearly sets forth the awfulness of sin. Many times people gloss over their sins and think of them only as mistakes or blunders; but the fact is that sin is a devilish thing, the very essence of everything that is bad, the antagonist of everything that is good. The devil takes every good blessing that God has given us, and when we yield our hearts to him, so that he can control us, he changes the good gift of God into a curse.

Take the gift of gold. How many blessings it brings to humanity! How it advances civilization! It makes art and literature possible. Used as the messenger of righteousness, as the servant of goodness, it relieves suffering; it dispels ignorance; it is the very angel of God. But once let the devil control the heart of him who has it, and it becomes the root of every evil and vicious thing. The old English poet, Chaucer, tells us of three boon companions who went out once on a time, in order to find and look at Death. And they met a wise old man, and asked him where they would find Death, and the old man said: "If you will follow the path through the wood, very soon you will come upon him." And the three young men went on the path through the wood, and very soon they came to a great pile of glittering gold. They had met Death, tho they knew it not. This is how it happened: They agreed that two of them should keep watch and ward over the treasure while the third went to the town to get the means of carrying it away. When the one was gone, the two began to talk together, and said, "If we were to make way with that third, there would be more treasure for each of us." And while the younger man was in town, the devil put it into his heart to reflect, "If I were to make way with those two, I should get all the treasure for myself." Accordingly he went into the stores and purchased food; he bought a bottle of wine and put poison in it, and came back to his friends in the wood. When they saw him coming, they overmastered him and killed him, and then sat down to regale themselves on the food that he had brought before they carried away their treasure. After eating of the food they drank the poisoned wine, and they, too, fell dead upon the heap of gold. And so what had been hailed by them as a great blessing, and what might have been a great blessing to them if they had possessed their hearts in honor and goodness, became their curse and their destruction when they yielded their hearts to the leadership of Satan.

The same thing is true of the fruits and food-cereals, with the seeds of which God has filled the earth. Nothing is of greater blessing to mankind than the vine with its grapes, or the tasseled corn with its yellow ears, or the waving fields of wheat and barley; but when the devil possesses the owner's heart and fills it with greed, or inspires in him a thirst for intoxicating stimulants, so that he changes the wheat and corn and grapes into intoxicating beverages, how soon the blessing becomes a curse!

Two young men walking down the street one evening in New Orleans saw a tramp looking with evident longing at the bottles in a saloon window. The young men were well-dressed, well-to-do fellows about town, and one of them said to the other, "Come, let us give this tramp a drink." They invited him in, and as with trembling hand he poured his glass full of liquor, one of the young men exclaimed: "Stop! make us a speech. It is a poor liquor that doesn't unloosen a man's tongue." The poor wreck of a man, ragged and dirty, clutched the glass of liquor in his hand and, lifting it to his thirsty lips, gulped it down greedily. As the fiery fluid coursed through his blood, he straightened himself, and stood before them with a certain grace and dignity which all the evidences of dissipation and all his rags and dirt could not obscure. "Gentlemen," he said, "I look to-night at you and myself, and it seems to me I look upon the picture of my lost manhood. This bloated face was once as young and handsome as yours. This shambling figure once walked as proudly as yours, a man in the world of men. I, too, once had a home and friends and position. I had a wife as beautiful as an artist's dream, and I dropped the priceless pearl of her honor and respect in the wine-cup, and, Cleopatra-like, saw it dissolve, and quaffed it down in the brimming draught. I had children as sweet and lovely as the flowers of spring, and saw them fade and die under the blighting curse of a drunkard father. I had a home where love lit the flame upon the altar and ministered before it, and I put out the holy fire, and darkness and desolation reigned in its stead. I had aspirations and ambitions that soared as high as the morning stars, and I broke and bruised their beautiful wings, and at last strangled them, that I might be tortured with their cries no more. To-day I am a husband without a wife, a father without a child, a tramp with no home to call his own, a man in whom every good impulse is dead. And all swallowed up in the maelstrom of drink." The tramp ceased speaking. The glass fell from his nerveless fingers and shivered into a thousand fragments on the floor. The swinging doors pushed open and shut again, and when the little group about the saloon bar looked up, the tramp was gone. But that was no exception, no rare case; it is what the devil is doing through strong drink to a hundred thousand men every year in the United States.

The thing which I want to impress upon you with all my heart is, that sin of any sort brings the man or woman who yields the heart to it into fellowship with the devil. Those who give Satan the right of way in their hearts become his servants. He is their master, and he directs what they shall do. How many times a man will fly into awful passion and utter wicked and cruel things, and if you ask him about it, he says, "I could not help it." The reason he could not help it is that he is no longer his own master, but, as the Scripture says, is "led captive by the devil at his will." A man promises himself that he will not fall again into his besetting sin, and when he finds himself again wallowing in it he says, "I could not help it." That is only another way of saying that he is not his own master. He has become the devil's vassal. He is the servant of sin. Left to himself, he is as helpless and as certainly ruined as tho he were already in hell.

But, thank God, that is not all our text. Jesus Christ came to destroy the works of the devil, and he will set us free if we will give him a chance to do it. But he will not do it against our will. If we ask we shall receive; if we knock it shall be opened unto us; if we seek we shall find; but there is not a single promise in the Bible of divine help without appropriate action on our part. I think there is a good deal of danger of deception on the part of some who think they must wait for some overpowering feeling to sweep them into a Christian life whether they will or no. There would be no virtue in repentance if it were forced on you.

A LOATHSOME RELATIVE. 123

You must choose Christ of your own free will. It is right for us to tell you of the good news of salvation, and persuade you with all the reasoning power and all the earnestness and love that we have; but you yourself must deliberately break with the devil, and choose Christ because it is right to do it, in order to your salvation. It is folly to wait for more feeling. What you need is to act in obedience to Christ. I do not want to excite you. I have never in my life sought to win any one to Christ by excitement. I want you deliberately to choose Christ as your Savior.

A celebrated English evangelist relates that when he was a young man, in Cornwall, England, there was a band of young men who worked together in the same mine, and who were great friends. In a time of revival these young men attended a series of meetings, and tho many others were converted, none of these young men made a start for the Christian life. One evening there fell upon that section, altho it was in December, and thunder was very rare at any time, a most terrific thunder-storm. It seemed that the full force and fury of the storm burst over the little church where the meetings were being held. The vivid flashes of lightning played across the faces of the crowd, illuminating the room with a weird and ghastly light. Great fear fell upon many in the congregation. It was a most overwhelming and indescribable scene. The thunder and lightning continued, peal after peal, flash after flash, the whole building vibrating at each fresh explosion. One by one those young men, who had been so long halting between two opinions, dropped on their knees, and from one after another the cry arose, "God be merciful to me, a sinner." Ere the storm ceased, all except one of that little band of friends had made a confession of conversion. This young man, Johnson Greenfell, was urged to yield. But he drew himself up with an air of dignity that might have done credit to a nobleman instead of a miner, and replied: "No, no, I will never stoop to this. If I give my heart to God, I give it; if to-night I were to bend my knees and ask God to have mercy upon me, I should simply be doing so because I am not master of my own actions, under the influence of fear. But," he added, "I will tell you what it is. By God's help, I will never again go through what I have gone through to-night. I have been trembling over the brink of hell, and if the Judgment Day is coming, if it dawns upon us now, I am a lost soul; but if God Almighty spares me till to-morrow, and I am in possession of my health and senses, my resolve is fixed. To-morrow, if God spares me, I will act in calm reason, and if God will have mercy upon my soul, I will seek his mercy till I find it." The evangelist declares that it was the only case in his whole career where he had occasion to be thankful at a man's putting off the salvation of his soul for one day. The next day came. He said to the young man, "Well, Johnson, what is it going to be?" "Oh!" he replied, "it shall be as I said last night." They knelt in the young man's room, and he confessed to God how he had trifled with his grace, how he had sinned against conviction. He thanked God he had not been cut off the night before, and there and then he gave his whole heart to God, and the peace of God came into his soul. The result of all this was that within six months from that night every one of those young men who had confessed Christ under the influence of their terror, and under stress of great feeling, had gone back into sin; while the young man who gave his heart to Christ because he knew it was the right thing to do remained steadfast and unmovable for the Lord. Don't let the devil deceive you into waiting for more feeling. Feeling will not save you. Christ can save you, and he will if you obey him. Confess him to-night and leave the result in his hands. No man has ever had cause to regret doing that.

XIV.

A LOVE STRONGER THAN LIFE.

Hereby know we love, because he laid down his life for us.—*1 John* iii. 16 (*Revised Version*).

CHRIST is the supreme manifestation of love in the history of the world. Other men have mastered themselves for their own selfishness; but he, for those who had given him no cause for love. A Roman senator related to his son that great honors were decreed to a number of soldiers whose names were written in a book, and the son became very importunate to see that book. The father showed him the outside; it seemed so glorious he desired him to open it; but the father replied: "No, by no means; it was sealed by the council." "Then," said the son, "tell me if my name is there." "The names are secreted to the Senate," replied the father. The son, studying how he might get some satisfaction, inquired of the merits of those inscribed soldiers. The father related to him the noble achievements and worthy acts of valor by which they had immortalized their names. "Such are written," said he, "and none but such must be written in this book." The son, consulting with his own heart, knew that he had no such trophies to show, but had been spending his time in foolish and wicked dissipation. But after seriously thinking the matter over, he deliberately made up his mind to change the whole course of his career, and became temperate and valiant. When the soldiers came to receive their wreaths, he stepped in to challenge one for himself. Being asked upon what title, he answered, "If honors be given to conquerors, I have gotten the noblest conquest of all." "Wherein?" was inquired in astonishment. "These have subdued strange foes," was his answer, "but I have conquered myself." This young soldier achieved mastery over himself for his own honor and glory; but Jesus Christ, who had honor and glory with the Father before the morning stars sang for joy, emptied himself of the glory of heaven and gave his life on the cross as a ransom for us.

Jesus Christ has made giving to be forever a greater glory than getting. Many years ago Frederick William III., the king of Prussia, was carrying on expensive wars. He was trying to strengthen his country and make a great nation of the Prussian people, and he had not money enough to accomplish his plans. What should he do? If he stopped where he was, the country would be overrun by the enemy, and that would mean terrible distress for everybody. He therefore appealed to the women of Prussia, as many of them as wanted to help the king, to bring their jewelry of gold and silver to be melted down into money for the use of their country. Many women brought all the jewelry they had, and for each ornament of gold or silver they received in exchange an ornament of bronze or iron, precisely like the gold or silver one, as a token of the king's gratitude. These iron and bronze ornaments all bore the inscription, "I gave gold for iron, 1813." They became more highly prized than the gold or silver ornaments had been, for they were a proof that the women had given up something for their king. It became very unfashionable to wear any jewelry. So the Order of the Iron Cross grew up, whose members wear no ornament except a cross of iron on the breast, and give all their superfluous money to the service of their fellow men. But our Savior did a greater thing than that. He did a greater thing than to give gold for iron. He laid down his life as a ransom for a race that was in rebellion against him, who not only did not give him love and gratitude in return, but abused him and insulted him, and crowned him with thorns, and persecuted him to the cross.

In coming down to earth and taking upon himself our flesh, Jesus Christ did the most knightly and chivalric deed the world has ever seen. All other illustrations of chivalry seem weak beside it. The story is told that when Mahomet II. besieged Belgrade, in Servia, one of his captains at last got upon the wall of the city and raised the colors of the invader. A noble Bohemian, seeing it, ran to the captain, and, clasping him fast about his middle, cast himself down headlong with the Turkish captain in his arms, and so by his voluntary death saved the lives of all in the city. But Jesus Christ came and dared the hosts of hell, and gave his life, not for those who admired and loved him, but for those who hated him or were indifferent to him—laid down his life for his enemies. Chivalry is full of tales of men who fought for their friends; but Christ went to his death for his enemies.

This wondrous love of Christ for us ought to awaken in our hearts the sincerest gratitude and love for Christ. Our ingratitude is a most unnatural thing. Even wild beasts have the instinct of gratitude. There is a famous classic story of one Androcles, a slave, dwelling in Rome, who fled from his master into the wilderness and took shelter in a lion's den. The lion came home with a thorn in his foot, and, seeing the man in the den, reached out his foot, and the man pulled out the thorn, which the lion took so kindly that for three years he fed the man in his den. After three years the man stole out of the den and returned back to Rome, was arrested by his master, and condemned to be devoured by a lion. It so happened that this very lion had been captured and was designed to devour him. The lion knew his old friend, and would not hurt him, but fawned upon him and confessed his affection for him in the most touching manner. The people wondered at it; the man was saved, and the lion given to him, and came to follow him about the streets of Rome. How many thorns Christ has taken out of our lives! what infinite love he has shown for us! And have we done as much as this grateful beast in return for his wonderful love?

The love of Christ is so great that it is sufficient to overcome the most sinful and wicked heart, where his gracious influence is given the right of way. Mrs. Paull was accustomed to go to the canal-boats at Delaware City, and carry illustrated papers to the women and children that she met on the boats. One day, on one of the boats, a bright little boy attracted her attention. He was sitting on a coil of rope, absorbed in reading. She gave him a picture card, containing on it a Scripture text, and some papers. The boy was delighted. Just then there issued from the cabin windows the sound of altercation and such a storm of abuse and vituperation that she involuntarily retreated before it. A man came out of the cabin and walked sullenly away. A woman's voice was still heard from within. Presently the woman appeared at the door, uttering horrible oaths and curses, and sent the boy for liquor. With a prayer in her heart for guidance, Mrs. Paull timidly knocked at the door of the canal-boat. The woman brusquely offered her a seat. With ready tact and true sympathy Mrs. Paull soon won her confidence, and by a few simple inquiries learned her story. She was ill with consumption, and the life on the water was hastening her end; but her husband would not permit her to live on shore. The poor woman had seen a great deal of sorrow. Her only daughter had been burned to death before her eyes. She had lost a baby also. Now only her boy remained to help or care for her. Night after night she lay and coughed, with no one to do anything for her. Mrs. Paull, with tears of sympathy, took the hard, toil-roughened hand, and as lovingly as one sister might plead with another told her of the love of Christ for her. On leaving she said, "Will you not sometimes think about what I have been saying?" "I shall think about it quite as often as you will think about me," was the reply. "I shall think of you and pray for you every day," said Mrs. Paull. "Good-by." And she kept her promise.

Late in the fall a woman came off from another barge and sought Mrs. Paull at her home, and gave her the illuminated card which she had given to the boy, with this message from him concerning his mother: "She wanted you to have it and to know how much good it did her." "You never would have known her," the woman continued. "She used to be such a hard case that, tho we are rough enough ourselves, we did not care to have anything to do with her. But a change came over her all at once. She began a new life, and after a minister had been to see her, you wouldn't have known her for the same woman. It was a pleasure to do anything for her, she was that patient through all her suffering. She never lost a chance of begging every one to love the Lord and go to him for forgiveness. You couldn't refuse her, she was that earnest; we can't none of us be like we were before she died. When the end came she looked as peaceful and as happy as if she were a little tired child going to sleep. I was sitting by her, holding her hand, when she opened her eyes and smiled at her husband and little boy. Then she says, very softly, 'For he careth—for he careth'; and that was the last she ever said."

Ah, if you will give your heart all to Christ and enter into the full joy of his love, the consciousness of his love will seem greater to you than all the other treasures of life.

When Henry IV., king of France, was told of the king of Spain's large dominions, he comforted himself in reply by saying: "But I am king of France; he is king of Castile, but I am king of France; he is king of Navarre, but I am king of France; he is king of Naples, but I am king of France; he is king of the West Indies, but I am king of France." He thought the kingdom of France was equivalent to all of the others. So the Christian rejoicing in the conscious love of Jesus Christ may say: "One has more wealth than I, but Christ is my lover; one has more learning or wit, but I am a Christian; one may have greater honor or a higher social position, but

I am glorified by the friendship of Jesus Christ my Lord; others may have a more pretentious dwelling-place here, but I have a mansion that is furnishing for me in heaven."

Let your heart yield itself to this boundless love of Christ for your soul, and enter even to-night into the joy of that divine inheritance which gives you the right to be a child of God and to have fellowship with Jesus Christ.

XV.

THE TESTIMONY OF THE DIVINE GUEST.

> And this is his commandment, that we should believe in the name of his Son Jesus Christ, and love one another, even as he gave us commandment. And he that keepeth his commandments abideth in him, and he in him. And hereby we know that he abideth in us by the Spirit which he gave us.— *1 John* iii. 23, 24 (*Revised Version*).

SURELY God could not have devised a more satisfactory way of assuring us of the certainty of our conversion and the divine quality of our experience than that which is set forth in this text. We have given here three distinct reasons for our Christian assurance: First, we believe in and keep the commandments of Jesus Christ; second, we are drawn out in sympathy and in love toward other friends of Jesus; we like to be with that kind of people; and, finally, the supreme testimony is that the whole spirit of our lives is changed. A new spirit has come into us and possessed us. The spirit of life has been transformed. This new spirit changes our attitude toward the Bible, toward prayer, toward other Christians, and toward Christ. After all, the supreme test as to whether a man is a Christian or not is in the question, "Does he have the Christian spirit?"

The theme which I specially wish to emphasize on your thought is this testimony to Christianity in the changed spirit of a life. In giving ourselves to Christ we insure the Holy Spirit's coming into our lives and causing our whole attitude toward God and Christ and heaven to be different. This will all come out very clearly if you will take some of the illustrations which are given us in the Bible, showing the changed spirit which comes over men when they are converted.

Take Paul's case. He hated Christians. It delighted him to see them suffer for their fidelity to Christ. But when that day on the road to Damascus he had a vision of Jesus, and heard that heavenly voice saying unto him, "Saul, Saul, why persecutest thou me? It is hard for thee to kick against the goad," his whole spirit of life was transformed; he began to pray, and forever afterward loved the society and fellowship of Christian people. His intellect was not changed, his body was not changed, his financial and other relations were just the same; but a new spirit had come in and taken charge and control of his life.

Take the case of blind Bartimæus, the man whom Jesus healed on his way to Jericho, the day he met Zacchæus. The old blind man sits begging by the wayside, when he hears the noise of the coming crowd, and he asks of somebody near, "Who is it?" And they tell him that Jesus of Nazareth passeth by. "What! Jesus of Nazareth, the great miracle-worker, he who healed the blind man and the leper? Then now is the chance of my life." And he shouts as loud as he can, until his shrill voice rises far above all other noises, "Thou Son of David, have mercy on me!" Indeed he shouts so loud that the bystanders turn on him in contemptuous indignation, and cry, "Hold thy peace." "What for?" he asks. "This is my only chance. I could afford to keep quiet when he was in Jerusalem and I had no way to get to him; but now that he is within reach of my voice, I shall not hold my peace. He will be out of hearing in a minute or two." And again the piercing cry of the blind man cuts the air, louder than ever, "Thou Son of David, have mercy on me!" By this time the crowd that follow after Jesus are getting close, and twenty men, I doubt not, shout, "Tell that blind beggar to be quiet." But I can hear him say: "It's all well enough for you that have got your sight, and can go along with him, and be introduced to him, and ask him politely and quietly for what you want, to tell me to keep still; but this is my only chance." Again he cries, "Thou Son of David, have mercy on me!" "Hold thy noise," says an indignant man. "The Master is busy talking to his disciples. Your case is hopeless anyhow. A man as old as you are, that was born blind, there is no sense in your calling after him and making a nuisance of yourself." But now the blind man's quickened sense of hearing tells him that the critical moment had come; the procession has come up to him, in a moment it will have passed by, and his chance will have been lost. So he pays no attention to the sneers of anybody, but shouts again, and this time there is a note of heart-break in it; there is in it the wail of the almost hopeless man who has suddenly been roused to feel that the one chance of his life is going by—"Thou Son of David, have mercy upon me." All he could do was to cry. The leper could see and could run and jump in before him. Even the man possessed with devils had power to come into his presence; the poor sick woman who was healed of the issue of blood could work her way through the crowd till she could touch his robe; the Magdalen could bring her box of ointment into his presence, and wipe his feet with the hairs of her head; but poor old Bartimæus had only one way, and that was to shout— but that was enough, for it reached the ear and the heart of Jesus.

Jesus was talking to his disciples especially about the death that was to come to him as the Savior of the world; but not even this conversation could so take up his attention that he could not hear a man in sorrow. And so Jesus stopped and said, "Bring that man to me." And then the very people who had been telling him to shut his mouth, and keep still, veer about like weather-vanes and offer him an arm and say, "Be of good cheer, he calleth thee." The old blind beggar is the center of all observation, and they lead him up to the presence of Jesus. And Jesus says to him, "What wilt thou that I should do unto thee?"

O my friend, it is not God's will that needs changing, it is not the will of Christ that needs persuading; it is your will. All the love and wisdom and power of heaven were put at the disposal of this poor blind beggar. "What wilt thou that I should do unto thee?" And Bartimæus, trembling with excitement, says, timidly enough no doubt, now, "Lord, that I should receive my sight." Then Jesus laid his fingers on those sightless eyes and said, "Be open," and to the man, "Go thy way, thy faith hath made thee whole."

And then what did Bartimæus do? I have related the whole story to bring that out. Why, this is what he did: he "followed him, glorifying God." He became one of the friends of Jesus. From a grumbling old beggar he became a man full of praise and thanksgiving to God for his great mercy and goodness. A new spirit had come into the man. He had new eyes, indeed; but that was not so important as this new spirit that possessed him.

Now the message that I have for you who are not Christians is this: The Lord is passing by; he has blessed one, and another, and another, and still others, in this series of meetings. He has changed their spirit as surely as he did that of Paul, or the blind man. And he is ready to do the same for you.

In every nook of the world the power of the Gospel is the same. In Cuba, one night, Diaz, the Cuban missionary, was holding a meeting, when a drunken man came in and sat, seemingly indifferent, through the service. Mr. Diaz was telling the story of Christ's love—that old, old story that is ever new. At the close of the service this drunken man, who had sobered up a little, came up to the pulpit and said to the preacher, "Does that man love me?"

"What man?"

"Why, that man you spoke about. Does he love such a wretch as me?"

"Oh, yes," said Mr. Diaz, "Jesus loves you, and wants you to come to him and be saved."

He gave him a New Testament and told him to read it. The next Sunday he came, well dressed, sober, and with the Testament in his hand. Soon he gave himself to Christ, and became an earnest and joyous Christian.

The man was a baker, and when Mr. Diaz went to call on him at his bakery he found that he had his Testament fastened to the wall, so that as he worked he could study the Word of God. A customer called him from the room, when Mr. Diaz turned and said to his wife, "Mrs. Fernandez, how do you like your husband being a Christian, and studying the Bible?"

"Oh, it has been a blessed change," she answered. "He used to come home drunk late at night, and curse and beat me. But now his whole spirit is changed, and he reads and sings and prays and lovingly gives me all I need." Then catching up the Testament, she kissed it, and said with tearful eyes, "Since that book came into this house I am a happy woman."

Thank God for the testimony of the Divine Guest that lives in the Christian heart!

That Guest will never desert us, but will cheer us and sustain us amid all the trials of life. In an English coal mine a boy about fifteen years old was working beside his father, who was a Christian man and had brought up his family to trust God. Both the father and the son carried a pocket Bible with them to their work. One day they were working together in a newly opened section of the mine, and the father had just stepped aside to procure a tool, when the arch above suddenly fell between them, so that the father supposed his child to be crushed. He ran toward the place and called to his son, who at length responded from under a dense mass of earth and coal.

"My son," cried the father, "are you living?"

"Yes, father; but my body and legs are under a rock."

"Where is your lamp, my son?"

"It is still burning, father."

With tears running down his face, the old man asked one other question, "What are you doing, my dear son?"

"I am reading my Bible, father, and the Lord strengthens me."

Those were his last words before God took him home.

Thank God for the testimony of the Divine Guest in our hearts!

This is what I come offering you to-night. He will transform your life and bring you into blessed fellowship with Jesus. Dr. Wharton, of Baltimore, was once holding a meeting in a Southern city, when there came forward one night a man in the last stage of drunkenness. He wore a very shabby suit of clothes and looked the picture of despair. When asked why he had come, he said, "Can Jesus Christ do anything for me?" Dr. Wharton told him that beyond doubt he could. The Christian people prayed for him and others, and he went away. A minister present told Dr. Wharton that he was the son of one of the most prominent men of that city; he had spent two fortunes, was a perfect outcast, and his wife and children were in want. Seven years passed away, and Dr. Wharton was in that city again. He received a letter one morning, asking him to come to a certain number on a certain street and take dinner with the man, who wished him to see "what God could do for a drunkard." He went, and found a beautiful little home, with a canary singing in its cage in a window. A bright-eyed little girl answered his ring, and informed him that the man whom he wished to see was her father, and lived there. In a few minutes the wife came in and welcomed him cordially; then husband and children came, and they sat and chatted pleasantly. After dinner, having spent a delightful hour, his host grasped his hand and said: "Wherever you go, I want you to tell the people what the Lord can do for a drunkard, and if you wish you may tell my name."

No matter what your sin, or how hopeless your case is in your own strength, Christ is able and willing to work the same transformation in you. The Holy Spirit will dwell in your heart, will purify your life, and make it beautiful with the spirit of heaven.

XVI.

THE BANISHMENT OF FEAR.

> There is no fear in love: but perfect love casteth out fear, because fear hath punishment; and he that feareth is not made perfect in love.—*1 John* iv. 18 (*Revised Version*).

LOVE and fear, in the sense in which fear is used in this text, are never fellow tenants in the same heart. If one comes in, the other moves out. They can not abide each other's company. It is not that they are not congenial only; they are deadly foes. Where one of them lives the other can not live. They can not breathe the same atmosphere. I think Matthew Henry is correct when he suggests that we must distinguish here between what is ordinarily called fear and being afraid. That is, between the fear of God, which means veneration of him, and a tender, loving fear of offending him and grieving him, and being suspicious that he will not care for us, or dreading him. There is a reverent fear which is consistent with perfect love; but there is a being afraid of God that arises from a sense of guilt, or from a doubt of his love toward us. It is this latter fear that can not live with love. John assures us that perfect love casteth out fear, and he declares that in so doing it casts out torment, for this sort of fear is a disquieting, torturing passion. Nothing can be more terrible, a more deadly foe to peace and happiness, than a suspicion or dread that God has forgotten us, or is indifferent to us, or that he is angry with us. This perfect love for Christ is a great smiling giant who can take this miserable fear by the throat and fling him out of the heart body and baggage.

John McNeill tells a very interesting story of his own boyhood in Scotland. He was working in the town several miles from home; but always on Saturday night, no matter how late he got through his work, he would walk home, so as to wake up at home on Sunday morning and spend the day with his father and mother. During the week he lived in lodgings in town. The road home was a very lonely one through a dreary glen. One Saturday night it was nearly midnight when he got through business and started to tramp six or seven miles over the lonely road home. The road had a bad name. It was the highway between one seaport and another, and there were ugly stories about men being knocked down and robbed. He was a young, nervous lad, of about seventeen, and it seemed to him in the darkness, every little while, that somebody was springing through a hedge at him. This particular night was very black, and two miles from his home the road got blacker than ever; a high wooded hill on the right, and another on the left, and no light from moon or star or kindly cottage window. He was just entering this dark defile, blacker than a wolf's jaw, and was hurrying, nervous and afraid, when suddenly he thought his heart would leave him, and then it came leaping back into him. About one hundred yards ahead, in the densest of the darkness, there suddenly rang out a great, strong, cheery voice, "Is that you, Johnnie?" It was his father, the bravest, strongest man he had ever known. He knew it was a black, gruesome night, and that the boy was nervous; and like a father he arranged to be waiting for him at the worst of it, at the gloomiest of it, at the very blackest of it, just where his fears would be worst and his nervousness greatest. The boy was thinking of the father away at home, sitting in the blaze and the ruddy glow of the fire, thinking of his boy trudging through the mire and the mud, when suddenly he cried out close to him. Even when he saved him from his fears he rather increased them for a moment. But when he had steadied himself and knew who it was, he felt he was as good as at home. For home is not merely four square walls, and John McNeill's home met him in the middle of that blackness and midnight darkness.

Is it not so with us, in life, many times? Are there not many here that could bear testimony that when you have been walking a dark and lonely path, and things have been getting very black and gloomy round about you, you have heard a voice greater than that of any earthly father cry, "Fear not, for I am with thee"? and lo! God's foot seemed rising and falling on the road beside your own.

Some of you here this morning are thinking of God as tho he were away off yonder at home, amid the glory and the splendor of heaven. You imagine he thinks about you once in a while, as you trudge along through the darkness and sin and mud down here in the world; but nevertheless he seems a long way off. He seems so busy to you also; you think of him as taking care of suns and moons and stars, and deciding the fate of nations and civilizations, until you think you are lost in the crowd and may never be found again, when really he is near to you. In the very darkest place he is near to you, ready to come to you. He is ready to come as Jesus came to his frightened, despairing disciples, walking on the waves in the storm in the night, and quieting them with his loving word: "Lo! It is I, be not afraid."

The way to get rid of this fear is to open your heart to his love and let your love go out to him. Fear will be thus banished in everlasting exile.

The most natural cause of fear of the tormenting sort is the consciousness of sin in the heart. If we get rid of sin by surrendering the heart to the love of God, fear goes out with the sin, and love comes in. Dr. J. Wilbur Chapman was preaching this great truth some years ago in a Western city, when the message took hold of a gentleman who had a reputable place in the community, was a teacher in the Sunday-school, and yet was an embezzler. He had kept, without being detected, for twelve years, a sum of several hundred dollars belonging to an Eastern firm by whom he had been once employed. He had gone West, covered up his transgression, and had tried to atone for it by a new life and by following honesty with all men. But that one sin, year after year, ate into his soul like a canker. The torturing fear engendered by it robbed him of all possibility of peace. As he listened to Dr. Chapman's sermon he sat trembling with fear, and his heart was crying out in the language of David, "My sin is ever before me." When the meeting was over, he went straight to the preacher, and told him his story, and then, following his advice, he went to Philadelphia, interviewed his former employers, restored the money, and put himself into their hands. They forgave the trespass, and he returned with a new joy in his heart. Love now came in and filled all his soul, and fear with its excruciating torment was banished. In this new joy he gave himself afresh to God, led his whole Sunday-school class to Christ, became a Christian worker of remarkable effectiveness, and when he met Mr. Chapman, years afterward, he took the preacher's hand and said, while tears of joy filled his eyes: "I have lived in heaven for six years—ever since my trespass was confessed and forgiven!"

There is no greater folly than for a man to suppose that he will be able to build up a happy and blessed life upon a basis of hidden sin. One of our poets has put one phase of this truth with peculiar force:

> "I dug a grave, and laid within
> Its hidden depths one secret sin.
> I closed the grave—and know full well
> That day I shut myself in hell!"

Surely no one could have more terrible torment than to live forever haunted by fears and suspicions that shut out peace and rest of the soul.

This wondrous love that casts out fear can always be had at the cross of Christ. Jesus, our Savior, is the source of our love, and we must light our love at his altar. Sir Walter Raleigh said that if all the pictures and patterns of a merciless, wicked prince were lost in this world, they might all again be painted to the life out of the story of King Henry VIII. But, on the other side, if all the mercy and sympathy and love were lost out of the hearts of men, these candles divine in our bosoms might all be lighted again at the heart of Jesus Christ. If all our love were extinguished, his love might easily rekindle it. Not a word that he spoke, not a deed that he did, not a passion that he suffered but serves to reveal his love. He brought love, he exercised love, he bequeathed love with his dying words, he died in the spirit of love—he is love.

THE BANISHMENT OF FEAR.

I should like, if I could, to be God's messenger to any who have known the joy and peace of this love of Jesus Christ, but whose hearts have grown cold, and because of that have been invaded again by tormenting fears.

An Eastern editor says that Leschetizky, of Vienna, is conceded even by his rivals to be one of the greatest, if not absolutely the greatest, teacher of piano-playing in the world. Paderewski, Slivinski, and others scarcely less famous have been his enthusiastic pupils. There is one event in his life that ought to have a significant message for us as Christians. He was for many years a distinguished performer at great concerts, and his annual tours were notable triumphs. But ten years ago, after playing one evening at Frankfort, he decided never to play as a performer again, and he has never done so. This is the way he tells the story at the conclusion of his evening at Frankfort: "The people shouted and cheered, and it was a real triumph. But I felt nothing at all in my heart, and it made me very sad. And when I got to my hotel I sat in a chair and thought about this instead of dressing for a banquet in my honor. And when the people summoned me to the banquet I excused myself and did not go, for I was too sad. And that night I resolved that since I could no longer feel what I played, I would never play again, and I never have."

Surely this experience of the great musician

ought to be full of teaching to many a backslidden disciple of Jesus Christ. Are there not many silent voices in our churches, that once were vocal with praise to God, who are silent now because they no longer feel the holy love glowing on the altar of their hearts? The love which once so warmed the soul that it involuntarily rushed to the lips for expression is not felt; they no longer speak because they no longer feel. There is no calamity so great as to lose the fervor and inspiration of that loving communion with Jesus Christ. No wonder the great musician was saddened when he no longer felt the thrill of his harmonies in his own heart; but it is an infinitely sadder thing when a Christian has lost the power to respond to the love of Jesus.

But, thank God, it is not hopeless; you may come back to your enthusiasm and to your joy by giving yourself up again to association and fellowship with Christ. There is no height of nobility, there is no richness of Christian experience, there is no glory of heaven, beyond the reach of the soul that surrenders itself completely to the love of Christ and thus banishes all fear from the heart.

Ella Wheeler Wilcox, who is ever growing, it seems to me, in spiritual insight as a poet, sings what I would to God we could all make the prayer of our heart of hearts:

"Show me the way that leads to the true life,
    I do not care what tempests may assail me,

THE BANISHMENT OF FEAR.

I shall be given courage for the strife,
  I know my strength will not desert or fail me;
I know that I shall conquer in the fray:
    Show me the way.

"Show me the way up to a higher plane,
  Where body shall be servant to the soul.
I do not care what tides of wo or pain
  Across my life their angry waves may roll,
If I would reach the end I seek some day:
    Show me the way.

"Show me the way, and let me bravely climb
  Above the grievings for unworthy treasures;
Above all sorrow that finds balm in time—
  Above small triumphs or belittling pleasures;
Up to those heights where these things are child's play,
    Show me the way.

"Show me the way to that calm, perfect peace
  Which springs from inward consciousness of right;
To where all conflicts with the flesh shall cease,
  And self shall radiate with the Spirit's light.
Tho hard the journey and the strife, I pray,
    Show me the way."

XVII.

LOVE'S RECIPROCITY.

We love, because he first loved us.—*1 John* iv. 19 (*Revised Version*).

THE supreme cause of love is the consciousness that we are loved by another. Christ's love for us arouses our love in return. Love is the mightiest conqueror in the world.

There was in the Army of the Potomac, in 1864, a man who was the terror of his company. He was disobedient, cruel, quarrelsome, and vicious. As a result he was often terribly punished; but there was no reformation. In due time, by the fortunes of war, a captain from another regiment was placed in command of that company. The first day the orderly sergeant informed the captain of the bad character of this man, he committed some misdemeanor, was arrested by a sergeant, and brought before the captain. He looked at him for a moment, and, speaking to the sergeant, said: "Let him go to his quarters."

"Shall I keep him under guard?" inquired the sergeant.

"Oh, no," said the captain, quietly.

That evening the captain called his sergeant and

said: "Go down to Mr. Blank's quarters and tell him to come up to my tent; I wish to see him."

"Shall I bring him under guard?" inquired the sergeant.

"Oh, no," said the captain. "Just tell him to come. I guess he'll come, if you tell him."

In due time the soldier stood inside the captain's tent, cap in hand. He was of fine physique, brave and daring.

"Take a seat, sir," said the captain.

The soldier obeyed, but all the time looking defiance.

The captain talked with him awhile about his home, his relatives, and such matters, and then said: "I have heard all about you, and thought I would like to see you privately and talk with you. You have been punished often; most times, no doubt, justly, but perhaps sometimes unjustly. But I see in you the making of a first-class soldier —just the kind that I would like to have a whole company of; and now, if you will obey orders, and behave as a soldier should, and as I know you can, I promise on my honor as a soldier that I will be your friend and stand by you. I do not want you to destroy yourself."

With that the soldier's chin began to quiver, and the tears trickled down his cheek, and he said: "Captain, you are the first man to speak a kind word to me in two years, and for your sake I'll do it."

"Give me your hand on that, my brave fellow," said the captain; "I'll trust you."

And from that day on there was not a better-behaved soldier in the Army of the Potomac. The gentleness and love of the captain had conquered him. They had conquered him because they had aroused his love. David says to God, "Thy gentleness hath made me great." God's infinite gentleness and love have inspired many another heart than David's to rise up out of the mire and clay and accept the strong hand stretched out to lift him up and place his feet again upon the Rock of Ages.

Nothing is more natural than that our love should respond to the love of Jesus for us. When we see the same thing in the family circle or among friends, we are not astonished at it. Mr. Moody tells the story of a boy in college, who was about to graduate. He wrote back to his mother on the farm, asking her to come and see him get his diploma. She replied that she could not do so. She said her clothes were worn, and she had no money to buy new ones for the occasion. She had already turned the skirt of her best dress once, and it was ragged on both sides. But he wrote the most tender letter of love, and told her how broken-hearted he would be if she were not there to enjoy his college honors, and assured her that her clothes would make no difference to him, and urged her to come anyway. The old woman went, dressed in her poor best, which was shabby enough. The commencement was in a fashionable church. The old woman's son was the honor man of his class, but he was prouder of his mother than of all his honors. He walked with her down the aisle to the center of the church and saw her into one of the best seats, and after a while, when he came out to deliver the valedictory, the tears ran like rain down the old woman's face. The president of the college came out and pinned a badge of honor on his coat; then something happened that was not on the program, but that interested everybody in that house more than all the eloquence of the day. The young man deliberately walked down off the stage and went directly to his mother. He dropped on his knee before her in reverence and took off the badge and pinned it to her faded dress. There were not only tears in his eyes, but in every eye in that vast audience, when he finished the little ceremony by bending over and kissing her wrinkled cheek. That was his testimony to the love and fidelity of that noble mother, whose hard toil and self-sacrifice had helped him through college.

Now we say that was natural; we feel that it was right and praiseworthy; but what shall we say of our duty toward Jesus Christ, our Savior; he whose love brought him down from heaven, to be born in the manger of Bethlehem; he whose love for us drove him to the place where they scourged him and crowned him with thorns, and crucified him on the cross. Could there be anything more natural than that our hearts should melt in love before his wonderful sacrifice for us? Indeed, does it not seem unnatural and ungrateful, almost beyond comparison, when we see a man or a woman turn away from the cross of Jesus Christ with a hard heart and a sneering or an indifferent look? Hard indeed must be the heart that feels the rising of no answering love to the unexampled love which Christ has shown for us.

I wish I knew how to make this love of Christ seem personal to every one of you here. There is a way of thinking about Christ's atonement as made for the whole world in such a way as to cause it to seem indefinite and vague, and without personal application to ourselves. But we are assured that Christ tasted death for every man. As Dr. George Pentecost says, God is a father, and tho he has a very large family, he loves each one of this great family with all his love. The blade of grass springing up on the lawn in May does not have just a little bit of the sunshine; it has all the light and heat and power there are in the sun. You may take a burning-glass, a double convex lens; it is nothing if you do not adjust it. You may put your hand out into the blazing sunlight of June, and it falls on you without great heat; but if you put the burning-glass between the sun and your hand, and draw it up or down until the light is focused into a point the size of a pinhead, it will set you on fire. So the love of God, which is like universal sunshine, is easily appropriated by each one of us if we will approach God's love through the Divine Burning-glass. God's love is concentrated in Jesus Christ. The heavenly voice said to John the Baptist, "This is my beloved Son, in whom I am well pleased." All the saving power of God's love centers in Jesus Christ, and if you come to Christ in penitence and faith you have brought to bear on your heart the personal love of God, burning into your heart through all that Jesus is and all that he has done. Men who try to live in the love of God may and do often feel a great deal of pleasure in the providence of God over them, which comes in the way of the good things of the earth, which falls like the rain upon the just and the unjust; but no man ever gets the saving power in his heart until it comes burning through the cross on which Jesus Christ died for his sin.

I appeal to you in the name of his great love for you to surrender your heart to him now.

XVIII.

LOVE'S EASY HARNESS.

For this is the love of God, that we keep his commandments and his commandments are not grievous.—*1 John* v. 3 (*Revised Version*).

THE highest credentials of love are to be found in obedience. The love that incarnates itself in service for the one beloved can never be doubted. It is idle to say that we love Christ unless we do the things that are pleasing to him. Paul says: "Tho I bestow all my goods to feed the poor, tho I give my body to be burned, but have not love, it profiteth me nothing." It is love that gives value to sacrifice. Love is sweeter than the perfume of a gift of flowers. Love weighs heavier than the gold bestowed upon the poor. Love is more nourishing to the soul than the bread fed to the hungry is to the body. Charity is only patronage until love touches it, and then it becomes divine sympathy.

The theme of our text, to which I wish specially to lead your thought, is the power which love has to take all the pain and suffering and hardness out of self-denial in our service for Christ. Many people when they are asked to be Christians shrink back because they feel it is a hard way. They have looked altogether on the things that are to be given up, and have not beheld or obtained a proper conception of the beauty and blessing which glorify a Christian life. I am here this evening to make this assertion, that the Christian life is the transcendently happy life in this world; that genuine Christians are the happiest, most cheerful, and most hopeful people in the world. Life is sweeter to them than it is or can be to anybody else. While it is true that in order to be Christians we must deny ourselves anything that compromises us as the friends of Christ, and must share the fate of Jesus, standing by his banner, and going with him in adversity or prosperity, never wishing to be popular where he is unpopular, there is in the Christian's heart an inspiration of love that takes all the hardness out of such an experience and makes his life supremely joyous. In inviting you to be Christians I am not opening the door into a dark alley of midnight gloom, but into a beautiful garden where spiritual graces, such as hope and faith and love and gentleness and mercy and patience, fill the air with the perfume of heaven; a garden which stretches onward into a life that grows brighter and brighter unto the perfect day.

Love has a power to make commonplace things romantic and beautiful. A very wealthy merchant who lives in the suburbs of an Eastern city has about his stately mansion extensive grounds filled with rare and beautiful things. But one of the interesting characteristics of his landscape gardening is that he has a great many of the old-fashioned country flowers and plants. When he began to improve his grounds, he said to his wife: "I want flowers; not the new-fangled things of to-day, but the flowers of long ago." And they set their heads together as well as their hearts to find all sorts of odd and old-fashioned things, long since out of date and almost forgotten save by a few people who, like himself, kept a liking for the trees and plants and shrubs that made beautiful their childhood's home. And so, after a while, the most conspicuous points on the grounds were filled with flowering almonds, or trumpet-creeper, or hollyhocks, that reminded them of childhood and youth and mother. Love crowned them with a beauty that other eyes could never see. So, when we surrender our hearts to Christ, in the presence of his great love for us, love covers the prayer-meeting, and the Bible-reading, and the self-sacrificing service with a beauty and a glory that the worldling can not see.

Once arouse the devotion of the heart, and there are no impossibilities in the way of sacrifice. In the time of the Civil War, a generation ago, a regiment of soldiers from Massachusetts marched proudly down Broadway, New York, and the crowd who looked on and cheered them seemed to recognize in face and figure their inheritance from an ancestry that never knew when they were defeated.

They carried their heads, as well as the guns, with a certain aristocracy of principle and pluck descended to them from the Pilgrims who landed on Plymouth Rock. "How often can your State send out such a regiment?" inquired a New Yorker. "Once a week for months to come; and if we can't put down the rebellion, Massachusetts herself will go to the front," was the proud reply. It was the love of country and of the flag and of liberty that made hardship and bullets and death seem easy.

Love gives man power to sacrifice habits. Dr. Russell H. Conwell tells the story of a man who came to him and wanted to take a temperance pledge. He told Dr. Conwell that he had been a moderate user of wine, and it often appeared at his table. A few days before, however, his eleven-year-old son had been found in the back-yard dead drunk from the wine on his sideboard. He wanted to be able to go to his son and ask him to sign the temperance pledge, but rightly felt that he could not consistently do it until he had first signed the pledge himself. He wrote at the bottom of the pledge, "For my son's sake." Love made the sacrifice easy.

Love stirs the soul and makes earnestness the natural atmosphere of the heart. A gentleman was passing along by a river one day, near a town, and saw a large crowd assembled. When he had joined them, he found that a boy, who was bathing in the water just below the dam, had gone down. After some trouble his body was recovered. It was found that it was a young colored boy, whom no one seemed to know. As the gentleman passed down the way toward the town, he met several women who were rushing toward the scene of the accident. They made anxious inquiry; but all passed on greatly relieved when they found that it was a colored boy. That told them that it was not their boy. But at last he met a colored woman. "Was it a little colored boy?" she inquired. "Yes." "About twelve years old?" The man said he thought so. With one wild cry of anguish the woman bounded forward, and the man did not need to be told that she was the mother of a boy that answered that description. Her love made anything else but earnestness unnatural and impossible.

Love of Christ wins its way into the hardest hearts, and makes the work of doing it the sweetest work in the world. I heard the other day of a cultured Christian woman who went into a wretched slum to visit a sick woman. She found the children almost naked. There was no fire. The poor woman was very feeble, and almost too ill to move, and she was lying on rags in a corner. The whole place was very dirty. The first thing the visitor did was to bring food into the home; then she made a fire, and, having given them a good meal, she sent out for some soap and a scrubbing-brush, and set to and cleaned the whole place out. Then she made the woman as clean and comfortable as she could, washed the children, and combed their hair, and made them look cheerful and neat. When all had been made as clean as possible, she turned to bid the sick woman good-by, saying: "You will be all right for to-day. I will come again in the morning, and see how you get on. Don't worry, for I am going to see you well again." The woman wonderingly and timidly said, "If you please, won't you tell me who sent you?" The good woman replied, "The Lord Jesus Christ sent me." The sick woman answered: "The Lord Jesus Christ sent you? Well, look here, the next time you see him, you tell him from me he's a good 'un, he is."

Oh that God would help us that our loving devotion may so present Jesus Christ to every unconverted man or woman that knows us that they shall see his beauty and goodness!

There is no stone of difficulty so heavy but love will roll it out of the way.

Mrs. Josephine Butler had been asked to speak in a Rescue Home, where there were a number of poor despairing women, and as she arrived and went to the window with the matron, she saw sitting outside a wretched object, and she said, "Who is that?"

The matron answered: "She has been in the house thirty or forty times, and she has always gone away again, and nothing can be done with her, she is so low and hard."

But Mrs. Butler said, "She must come in."

The matron said: "We have been waiting for you and the company is assembled, and you have only an hour for the address."

Mrs. Butler responded, "No, this is of more importance"; and she went outside where the woman was sitting and said, "My sister, what is the matter?"

"I am not your sister," was the reply.

And then Mrs. Butler laid her hand on her and said, "Yes, I am your sister, and I love you"; and so she spoke until the heart of the poor woman was touched. The conversation lasted some time, and the company were waiting patiently. Finally Mrs. Butler brought the woman ino the room. There was the poor, wretched, degraded creature, full of shame. She would not sit on a chair, but sat down on a stool beside Mrs. Butler's seat, and that great woman let her lean against her, and kept her arm around the poor woman's neck while she spoke to the crowd of people. And that love touched the woman's heart and worked out her salvation. She had found one who really loved her, and love gave access to the love of Jesus.

Now the love of Christ made it easy for Mrs. Butler to do that. There is not a woman on earth who is not a Christian who could have done it; but the love of Christ in her heart, her consciousness of Christ's great love for her, made it possible for her to do it with all gladness.

I call you to the most joyous life in the world; a life of forgiveness and of peace. Turn away from every sin and give yourself up to this sweet and loving life to-night!

XIX.

MAN'S GREATEST VICTORY.

For whatsoever is begotten of God overcometh the world: and this is the victory that hath overcome the world, even our faith. And who is he that overcometh the world, but he that believeth that Jesus is the Son of God?—*1 John* v. 4, 5 (*Revised Version*).

PAUL names faith first among the three graces that are to abide forever, tho he declares that love is still greater. Faith is the eye of the soul. The author of Hebrews declares that it is "the assurance of things hoped for, the proving of things not seen."

It is not only in religion that faith is a dominant and necessary quality. Unbelievers sometimes talk as tho Christianity was unnatural and unreasonable in making so much of faith. But Christianity does not make any more of faith than the Chamber of Commerce does, or the Stock Exchange. Faith is just as essential a factor in the financial world as it is in the spiritual world.

A man said to Mr. Moody a while ago:

"Moody, the doctrine you preach is most absurd; you preach that men only have to believe to change the whole course of their life. A man will not change his course by simply believing."

Mr. Moody said: "I think I can make you believe that in less than two minutes."

"No, you can't," he said; "I'll never believe it."

Mr. Moody said: "Let us make sure that we understand each other. You say a man is not affected by what he believes, it will not change his course."

"I do."

"Supposing," said Moody, "a man should put his head in at that door and say the house was on fire, what would you do? You would get out by the window if you believed it, wouldn't you?"

"Oh," he replied, "I didn't think of that!"

"No," the great evangelist said quietly, "I guess you didn't."

Faith is at the foundation of all society, of commerce, of everything else.

Faith is a source of that enthusiasm of life which overcomes what otherwise would be impossibility.

Dr. Stalker, of Glasgow, remarks on the change in value of that word "enthusiasm." People used to be warned against enthusiasm. I have a book in my library by a great man in his day, and have sermons by so famous a man as Dr. South, warning against enthusiasm. The history of words is very interesting. A word that is despised in one age often comes to be a special favorite in another. One hundred and fifty years ago in English literature "enthusiasm" was a term of contempt. We are coming now to understand the value of enthusiasm. It is born of the three great principles of faith, hope, and love. Its chief source is in faith. It has the power to overcome the world. It is more important in an army than thousands of men. Faith in a leader may mean all the difference between glorious victory and shameful defeat. That is the secret of the remarkable victories achieved a hundred years ago by the first Napoleon. Every Frenchman believed in Napoleon, in his military genius—that he was invincible in battle. The young men of the country were ready to risk body and soul on their faith in him. This faith wrought wonders. When he went through the hospital, even the sick and dying sprang up as if new life had been put into them by the very sight of him; and if he was in danger of his life there were hundreds ready to thrust themselves between his body and danger. On the day of battle the men believed that he would certainly lead them to victory, and that faith made them win the victory.

It is that same enthusiasm of faith, lifted up and exalted into the spiritual realm, that gives men and women victory over the world. Many people when urged to be Christians think about the duties of a Christian life with reference to their own strength to resist evil, and they say: "I could not hold out; the sinful, wicked world is too strong; it would overcome me and defeat me in disgrace."

But that is leaving out Christ. If you will think of his power and his wisdom and love, and throw that into the balance, it will outweigh everything on the other side.

Plutarch tells us that Antigonus, king of Syria, being ready to give battle near the Isle of Andreos, sent out his squadron to watch the motions of his enemies and to descry their strength. Return was made that they had more ships, and better manned than his own. "How?" said Antigonus. "That can not be; for how many dost thou reckon me?" That brave man rightly felt that his own daring and skill, coupled with the faith that his men had in him, outweighed the larger numbers of the enemy.

The man who gives himself to be a soldier of Jesus Christ allies himself with the valor, the experience, and the power of his Lord. Every true Christian can say with Paul, "We are more than conquerors through him that loved us."

There is no doubt or fear or threat of the world that can defeat the soul that gives itself to Christ in the frank confidence of childhood.

There is a story of a poor man who was passing through a very trying experience. And a self-sufficient and bad-humored doctor came along and said to him:

"Good-morning, poor man."

"I never had any bad morning," said the sorely tried man.

"No?" said the doctor. "You are a miserable,

poor man; you are ragged, and without friends; there is no prospect of your troubles being relieved; how can it then be true, what you say, that you never had any bad morning?"

"I'll tell you," said the other. "Whether I am sick or in health, whether it be warm or cold weather, whether I be ragged or well clothed, rich or poor, I bless God for all."

"Oh, but, friend," said the doctor, "what if Christ should cast you into hell?"

"If he should, I would be contented; but I have two arms—the one of faith, the other of love—wherewith I would lay such fast hold on him that I would have him along with me, and then I am sure that hell would be heaven if he were there."

No wonder that with such a faith Paul could say, "All things work together for good to them that love God." Are there not those who hear me to-night, to whom it would be a blessed boon to drop all the burden of your sins at the foot of the cross, and face the future with the same sweet hope in your heart?

The soul whose faith is in Jesus Christ knows that there is no limit to the resources that have been set aside by the Divine love to supply all the needs of his nature.

Many years ago, in the days of Spanish wealth and glory, a Spanish ambassador, coming to see the famous Treasury of St. Mark, in Venice, dropped on his knees and groped at the bottom of the chests and trunks, to see whether they had any bottom; and being asked the reason why he did so, answered: "In this, among other things, my master's treasure differs from yours, in that his hath no bottom, as I find yours to have!" The proud Spanish ambassador was thinking of the mines of Mexico, Peru, and the West Indies. Spain has long since found the bottom even to that rich treasury. But, thank God, there is a treasury that can never be exhausted. Men's gold bags, purses, safety-vaults, and mints may be exhausted and drawn dry; even the Bank of England might become bankrupt; but the riches that are to be found in Christ Jesus have no bottom: his treasure vaults are bottomless; millions draw their hope and faith and love and courage from him, and he does not feel it at all. He is ever giving, and yet his storehouse is never empty. Paul was thinking of this when he said: "But my God shall supply all your need, according to his riches in glory by Christ Jesus."

There is abundance there for every one. Do not let the devil deceive you into doubting Christ's ability to supply all your needs. He can supply your need of goodness; he can strengthen you to resist evil; he can cleanse your heart from all your sins; he can liberate you from every sinful bondage; he can inspire you with hope unbounded; in him you may find your all in all. Give him your heart now, and begin this new life of victory.

XX.

WHAT IS IT TO LIVE?

He that hath the Son hath the life; he that hath not the Son of God hath not the life.—*1 John* v. 12 (*Revised Version*).

THERE is such a thing as life, and there is such a thing as "the life." Life in the sense of worldly sensation is a very brief and frail matter, but "the life" is clothed upon with immortality. This spiritual life, which is referred to in the text under the phrase "the life," can only come to us as the gift of God through Jesus Christ. It is what Paul is speaking about in his letter to the Romans when he says: "The wages of sin is death; but the gift of God is eternal life through Jesus Christ our Lord."

There can be no doubt that the plain, simple teaching of God's Word is that the only source of spiritual life which promises salvation is through Jesus Christ. No man will ever be saved on his own morality; every man, woman, and child who walk in the heavenly streets at last will agree upon one thing—that salvation is only through God's mercy and forgiveness.

Among the Hindus there is a strange tradition of a thief upon whom sentence of death had been passed, who, while in his cell, hit upon a plan which he determined to try as a scheme to save his life. He sent for his jailer and told him that he had a secret to impart to the king by which he might come into the possession of enormous wealth, but that he would only impart this secret in a personal interview. Word was taken to the king, who ordered the condemned man to be brought before him. The man informed his majesty that he knew the secret of making gold grow on a tree in the same way as fruit, and offered to make the experiment at once. The king was naturally anxious to profit by the man's knowledge, and, placing himself under his direction, accompanied by his chief minister, the high priest, and a few of his most favored courtiers, he went with the thief to a place outside the city wall. The thief selected a spot, and taking a gold coin from among his rags, said:

"If this be sown in the ground at this spot, then it will bring forth a tree upon the branches of which there shall hang golden fruit, like clusters of grapes upon a vine; but this will only happen on one condition: it must be planted by the hand of a man who has never been guilty of a single dishonest action. My hands are not clean, so I pass the coin to his majesty the king." The king then took the coin, and held it nervously in his fingers for a few seconds; then, as he passed it to his chief minister, he said: "I remember when I was young I took a small sum from my father's treasury, and therefore I think the chief minister should plant it." The minister, with words of caution, said: "Your Majesty, I should not like this most interesting experiment to be exposed to the possibility of failure through any oversight on my part; and as I receive the taxes from the people and am subjected to so many temptations, it is just possible that my hands are not altogether clean; so, with your royal permission, I shall pass it to the commander-in-chief of the army. But the general would have nothing to do with it. With military brusqueness he said: "No, no; I handle the army money, buy the rations, and pay the forces; give it to the high priest." But the old Hindu priest was not prepared to take the responsibility, and said: "You forget that I collect the tithes and allot the sacrifices; I can not take it." Then quickly up spoke the thief: "Your Majesty, why hang me as a thief when of the four highest men in the kingdom not one will answer for his own honesty?" The old legend says that the king saw the force of the argument and pardoned the thief. This, of course, may be but an idle story; but it suggests a great truth. In the language of Isaiah, "All we like sheep have gone astray; we have turned every one to his own way"; and our only hope is that God hath laid on Jesus Christ "the iniquity of us all." It is idle to dream of salvation without the forgiveness of sin.

Moody says that he met some time ago a man of

a self-righteous and boasting temperament, who claimed that he had never sinned in his life.

The preacher asked him, "Do you ever get angry?"

"Well," he said, "sometimes I do; but I have a right to do so. It is righteous indignation."

"Do you ever swear when you get angry?"

He admitted that he did occasionally.

"Then," the minister asked, "are you ready to meet God?"

"Yes," he replied, "because I never mean anything when I swear."

"Suppose," replied Moody, "I steal a man's watch and he comes after me. 'Yes,' I say, 'I stole your watch and pawned it; but I did not mean anything by it. I pawned it and spent the money; but I did not mean anything by it.'"

You would sneer at and hold in contempt such a statement. We can not trifle with God like that. You may depend upon it that no possible sham or lack of genuineness will pass at the Judgment. Unless your life and character are built upon true principles, and unless the life of heaven pulsates in your heart through the mercy of God in Jesus Christ, in the great day of trial you will go to pieces in collapse.

A new bridge had to be built across a deep ravine in the mountains through which, during winter and wet seasons, a large stream of water rushed. In summer and in dry seasons there was no water in it. After it was contracted for, a very convenient drought set in, much to the delight of the contractor and his men. It took many weeks to build; but at length, at six o'clock one evening, it was all finished except the keystone. That night the contractor said to his men: "Men, work overtime to-night, and get in the keystone; we don't know when the storm may come." The men replied: "No, there is not the shadow of a cloud in the sky; to-morrow will be fine"; and they flung down their tools and left. The contractor went home with the burden of a heavy foreboding of disaster lying on his heart. At five o'clock next morning the wind rose, the clouds gathered dark and thick, and before six o'clock a waterspout broke on the mountain-top; the ravine was flooded with water, which washed away the wooden supports of the bridge, and it fell—all for want of a keystone.

My dear friends, Christ is the true keystone of our lives. All the earthly supports that make so much show about us are like the wooden scaffolding of a bridge. In the storm of temptation, of sickness, of misfortune, or of death, they will be swept away, and unless Christ is the keystone of our character, unless his divine life is in us, we shall go down in ruin. Everything that is merely human and of this world will come to failure in the end. Only that which comes from Christ, which centers in him, shall have immortality and be beyond the power of decay.

Hogarth, the great artist, was one night in the midst of a convivial company seated about his own table in his house in London. Suddenly his brilliant intellect conceived the idea of his famous picture afterward known as the "Tail Piece," and he immediately announced the subject to his friends.

"My next undertaking," said he, "shall be 'The End of All Things.'"

"If that is the case," interrupted one of the party, "your business will be finished; for there will be an end to the painter."

Hogarth suddenly lost all his gaiety, and remained for some time plunged in the deepest gloom. At last he said, with a melancholy smile: "That will be so, and therefore the sooner my work is done the better."

The next day he began work on the picture, and worked with such diligence that his friends saw he feared he would not live to finish it. But the picture was finished, and in a wonderful manner. He grouped together there everything that could denote the end of all things—an old broom, worn to the stump; a broken bottle; a cracked bell; a bow unstrung; the butt end of an old musket; towers in ruins; a crown smashed in pieces; the falling signpost of a tavern called the World's End; the moon on the wane; the map of the world burning up; a gibbet falling, the body gone, and the chains that held it dropping down; Phœbus and his horses lying dead in the clouds; Time with his hour-glass and scythe broken; a vessel wrecked; a tobacco-pipe with the last whiff of smoke going out; a play-book opened, with "Exit all" printed in the corner; an empty purse; and a statute of bankruptcy taken out against Nature.

All this finished, Hogarth surveyed the picture for some time. Then he said, "Nothing remains but this," and taking up his pencil, he added a painter's palette broken.

"Finis!" he then exclaimed; "the deed is done; all is over." And he died.

That grim story of Hogarth is a fair illustration of the wreck and ruin that come to all things that are merely earthly. Our hold on everything worldly is but transient. The only life that can really give us satisfaction and peace is the life of the soul. Such a life is not affected by the end of earthly things. The dying hour to a soul filled with the life which Christ gives is but the entrance to the harbor of another world.

It is said that the last words that were read to Mr. Gladstone were these verses of Matthew Russell's entitled "The Dying Hour":

> "My dying hour, how near art thou?
> Or near or far, my head I bow
>   Before God's ordinance supreme;
>   But, ah! how priceless then will seem
> Each moment rashly squandered now!
>
> "Teach me, for thou canst teach me, how
> These fleeting instants to endow

> With words that may the past redeem,
> My dying hour!
>
> "My barque that late with buoyant prow
> The sunny waves did gaily plow,
> Now, through the sunset's fading gleam,
> Drifts dimly shoreward in a dream.
> I feel the land breeze on my brow,
> My dying hour!"

When John Quincy Adams was eighty years old, he was met one morning on the streets of Boston by an old friend, who, taking his trembling hand, said: "Good-morning! And how is John Quincy Adams to-day?"

"Thank you," the ex-President and devout Christian replied; "John Quincy Adams himself is well, sir; quite well, I thank you. But the house in which he lives at present is becoming dilapidated. It is tottering upon its foundation. Time and the seasons have nearly destroyed it. The roof is pretty well worn out. Its walls are much shattered, and it trembles with every wind. The old tenement is becoming almost uninhabitable, and I think John Quincy Adams will have to move out of it soon; but he himself is quite well, sir; quite well."

Who does not see the infinite superiority of such a conception of life as that! Surely John spoke truly when he said, "He that hath the Son hath the life." It is a life which we shall carry with us, or rather which shall carry us with it, back to the heaven from whence it came.

It is said that in one of the Eastern cemeteries a casket is lying in the receiving-vault awaiting the completion of a beautiful mausoleum which is being constructed for its permanent resting-place. Beside the casket is a music-box which is wound up every day by the widow of the man whose body is in the casket. She goes to the vault at the same hour daily, and sits there for an hour or two while the music-box plays his favorite tunes, and when she goes away her face shows that she has been weeping. She says that she has ordered for the new tomb a mammoth music-box from Switzerland, and that it will be a part of its interior furnishings. There is something infinitely pathetic and sad in that little picture. Alas! no human music can soothe "the dull, cold ear of death." But if we yield our hearts to God, if we enter into fellowship with Jesus Christ, then heavenly melodies shall fill our souls, and we shall not need a music-box in our tomb, for we shall carry divine music with us into that land where music was born. Yield Christ your heart now!

XXI.

A PROSPEROUS SOUL.

Beloved, I pray that in all things thou mayest prosper and be in health, even as thy soul prospereth.—*3 John* 2 (*Revised Version*).

This was the prayer of the great-hearted John, which he made for Gaius, one of the Christians who had been won to Christ through John's personal ministry. None but an earnest, true-hearted minister can perfectly understand John's feeling toward Gaius. If a man or a woman, no matter how many years afterward, comes to the true soul-winner and says to him, "It was you that turned me from my sins, and persuaded me to accept Christ as a Savior," there is established at once one of the tenderest possible claims for sympathy and attention. Greatly to be pitied is the minister who does not feel within him that which responds to these tender words of John when he says: "For I rejoiced greatly, when brethren came and bare witness unto thy truth, even as thou walkest in truth. Greater joy have I none than this, to hear of my children walking in the truth."

There is an old tradition related by Eusebius, that John, on a visit to a city in the neighborhood of Ephesus, commended to the care of the bishop a young man of fine stature, graceful countenance, and ardent mind as suited to the work of the ministry. The bishop neglected his charge. The young man became idle and dissolute, and was at length prevailed on to join a band of robbers such as commonly had their holds in the neighborhood of ancient Greek cities. He soon became their captain and attained a shameful eminence in crime. Long after, John entered the city again, and inquired for the young man.

"He is dead," said the bishop; "dead to God."

Having ascertained the particulars, John the Greatheart exclaimed, "I left a fine keeper of a brother's soul!"

The apostle mounted a horse, rode into the country, and was taken prisoner. He did not attempt to flee, but said: "For this purpose I am come; conduct me to your captain."

He entered the presence of the armed bandit, who, recognizing the apostle, tried to escape.

"Why dost thou fly, my son," said he, "from thy father—thy defenseless, aged father. Fear not; thou still hast hopes of life. I will pray to Christ for thee. I will suffer death for thee. I will give my life for thine. Believe that Christ has sent me."

The man was subdued, fell into the apostle's arms, prayed with many tears, and forever after lived a noble and pure life.

At the time of this letter of John to Gaius, and

of his aged friend's expression of love and sympathy, in which he reveals what is his prayer for him daily, Gaius was evidently sick, and John writes him this sympathetic love-letter to encourage and cheer him. He was a very good man, and John was wishing in his heart that the soul of Gaius and his body were better matched. His soul was large and robust and prosperous; adorned with every charming grace; while the body was weak and afflicted and racked with pain. With delicate sensitiveness to the situation, John prays that Gaius may be as prosperous and healthy in his physical life as he is in his spiritual health. What a blessed thing so to live that those who love us dare to pray that prayer for us!

The first suggestion which I wish to impress is that soul prosperity is a great deal more important than bodily prosperity. It is a great thing to have a healthy body. When we are sick and weak, we are likely to draw on the strength and good cheer of every one that associates with us; but, on the other hand, when we are strong and wholesome in our physical personality we seem to add something of stimulation and inspiration to others who are not so strong as we are. There is such a thing as radiating physical vitality, as a fire radiates heat, and we should thank God for health, and seek to keep it, as much for the helpfulness of others as for our own enjoyment. But if one must choose between a healthy body and a healthy soul, the prosperous, healthy soul is infinitely more to be desired. Many of the greatest people who have ever lived have conquered in the spirit of Dr. Watkinson, the ex-president of the British Conference, who used to say in his frail and sickly youth, "This soul of mine shall be master of this body of mine, or leave it." Florence Nightingale has been an invalid, shut up in a sick-room, nearly all her life; but what a conqueror she has been through the health of her soul! Mrs. Browning was a frail, delicate woman, always on the brink of departing from the body; but her soul was prosperous and splendid, and her songs have cheered the world for all time to come. William of Orange was so weak that the slightest exertion fatigued him, and he walked in the shadow of death during all the years of his manhood; but the majestic force of his will and the prosperity of his soul never fainted or was eclipsed. Lord Nelson never went to sea without being sea-sick. In all these and in thousands of others the soul was superior to the body and mastered it.

A prosperous, healthy soul can use poor and feeble instruments, and by the Divine help can make their soul-health have a wide reach of blessing. I went in my young ministry to a community that seemed all wicked and godless, save one woman who had had rheumatism that had kept her in her room for twelve years; she was the only person that kept up any testimony for Jesus Christ. I began to preach the Gospel in that community, and in ten days sixty-five men and women, many of them of the wickedest sort, had given their hearts to God and were organized into a flourishing church. It was largely a surprise to me. I had not had faith to warrant such a result. But when I went up on the mountain to see that sick woman, and looked in her holy face, chastened by suffering, glowing like an angel's with the presence of the Spirit Divine, and she told me that when she heard I was about to begin the meetings she had poured out her soul to God, day after day, for more than twelve hours out of twenty-four; and that many nights she had wet her pillow with her tears pleading for the Divine blessing on the young stranger-preacher and that salvation might come to the people,—I no longer wondered at the great success that had come seemingly through such feeble instrumentalities.

We can not all have large and imposing and healthy physical personalities; but every one of us may be spiritual giants. We may be prosperous and glorious in our souls. The spiritual graces may adorn and glorify our conversation, our thoughts, our deeds, and give us an influence that shall be heavenly wherever we go.

I wish to impress this other thought suggested by the Scripture we are studying, that it is a great test of our own character. What greater compliment could John have paid to Gaius than this prayer to God, that his friend's body should be as prosperous as his soul? If Gaius had been indifferent or half-hearted in his devotion to Christ, or if he had been a sinful man who gave Christ no testimony, a man diseased by sinful habits, whose heart was full of wicked lusts, a man of angry and vicious spirit, John would never have dared to utter such a prayer for him. To pray that a sinful man may be as healthy in his body as he is in his soul is to pray that his tongue may be parched with fever, his limbs racked with pain, and that deadly and loathsome disease may lay its death-like hand upon him.

There is a very solemn side to this question. I pray God we may have the honesty, each of us, to search our own hearts with this theme. Let each one personally put the question to himself: "Would I dare ask God to measure out to me my physical health by my spiritual health: would I be able to go about my business to-morrow, and do my work with a glad heart and buoyancy of spirit, if God should measure out my physical strength, my nerve force, measure by measure, with the spiritual vitality in my heart?" There is a question that may well make us pause. If we can not answer it in the affirmative, if there is a feeling of hesitancy and of danger in such a prayer, then there is no doubt what we need. We need the great Physician of souls. We need him who is able to cure the greatest disease, the disease of sin. We need the spirit that will cause us to cry out like the leper who came to Christ for cleansing, saying, "Lord, if thou wilt, thou canst make me clean." And the same Jesus who put forth his hand and touched him, saying, "I will; be thou clean," will pardon our sins and cleanse us from all unrighteousness. That poor leper was not more immediately cleansed than you will be if you will act with the same promptness and earnestness that characterized him.

Our one hope of spiritual healing is in Jesus. Anselm once wrote a tract containing "A Sinner's Plea." It began:

"Dost thou believe that the Lord Jesus died for thee?"

"I believe it."

"Dost thou thank him for his passion and death?"

"I do thank him."

"Dost thou believe that thou canst not be saved except by his death?"

"I believe it."

And then Anselm says to the sinful man: "Come, then, while life remaineth in thee; in his death alone place thy whole trust; in naught else place any trust; to his death commit thyself wholly; with this alone cover thyself wholly; and if the Lord thy God will to judge thee, say: 'Lord, between thy judgment and me I present the death of our Lord Jesus Christ; no otherwise can I contend with thee.' And if he shall say that thou art a sinner, say thou, 'Lord, I interpose the death of our Lord Jesus Christ between my sins and thee.' If he say that thou hast deserved condemnation, say: 'Lord, I set the death of our Lord Jesus Christ between my evil deserts and thee, and his merits I offer for those which I ought to have and have not.' If he say that he is wroth with thee, say: 'Lord, I oppose the death of our Lord Jesus Christ between thy wrath and me.' And when thou hast completed this, say again: 'Lord, I set the death of our Lord Jesus Christ between thee and me.'"

XXII.

THE CHRIST IN LIFE'S CLOUDS.

Behold he cometh with the clouds; and every eye shall see him, and they which pierced him.—Rev. i. 7 (*Revised Version*).

ALL Scripture converges to the truth that this life is a school-time of preparation for an immortal career which is to follow. What we are doing now is not only important as having reference to our character and our happiness in this world, but it is critical with relation to the life we are to live hereafter. We must meet our conduct again. How significant this statement that the Roman soldier who pierced Christ with his spear shall meet Christ again face to face! There is a world of revelation and teaching in that simple sentence. No sin is forgotten or buried because for the moment it seems to be lost out of sight. No good deed is lost in oblivion, tho for the present it seems to go unrequited.

I do not think it would be fanciful to-night for us to follow the beautiful imagery of this first sentence of our text, and remind ourselves that Christ's coming at last, in the clouds in judgment, is in harmony with the way he has always been coming.

The first coming of Jesus was in the clouds of poverty. He was born in the manger; he was not cradled in luxury, but in the hay of a stable. But all the poverty that surrounded that scene could not hide the fact that he was the Christ. Angels came and sung the happy secret to the shepherds out on the plains of Bethlehem, and they flocked to the little town to inquire and wonder and worship and go away with rejoicing. Wise men from the East sought out that little stall in the stable, and, bowing down to the earth, laid their rich gifts of gold and frankincense and myrrh at the feet of the Babe. The clouds of poverty were brightened and illuminated by the Christ in them. Thank God! it has ever been so. No man or woman has ever yet gone down into poverty's darkness where the clouds were so black that they were not illuminated if Jesus Christ were present. He can make poverty sweeter by far than riches are without him. He can give dignity and honor to the humblest of his disciples.

Dr. C. I. Scoffield tells a story of how, in the old slavery days, General A——, a man of great force of character, but not a Christian, was sick unto death.

His wife went to him, after talking with the doctor, and said: "Tom, the doctor says you must die, and I can not bear to see you die unsaved. Shall I send for my pastor to talk and pray with you?"

"No," said the dying man; "send for old Uncle Ben."

Ben was the plantation blacksmith, and a powerful exhorter whose holy life illustrated his doctrine.

When the old slave came in, General A—— said: "Ben, they say your old master has got to die; and, Ben, I am not fit to die; I can't die in my sin. What must I do?"

"Massa Tom," said the old man, solemnly, "I'se mighty sorry to see you so poorly; but, Massa Tom, you done been a great sinnah, and you must do some powerful repenten and b'lieven, ef you gwine to git you soul saved."

"Well, Ben," sobbed the dying master, "I will, I will. Now, Ben, you get right down here and pray for your old master."

Uncle Ben knelt by the general's bedside and poured out his heart with strong crying and tears to Him who is able to save. And when the prayer was ended, the two old men, the white master and the faithful black slave, were brethren in Christ Jesus. Christ was able to illuminate the clouds of poverty and slavery and glorify the old black slave.

Christ came in the clouds of persecution. Herod sought his death when he was a little child. He went down into Egypt hunted by the hand of a murderer. But wherever he went he was still the Christ. He is able to illuminate all the clouds of persecution that come about those who trust him.

There has never been a dungeon so dark but that Christ has been able to fill it with songs of gladness, as he did in the case of Paul and Silas at Philippi. There never has been a jail with locks so solid but that Christ has been able to send his angel to deliver, as he sent to Peter. There has never been a martyrdom so cruel but that Christ has been able to send such joy to the heart as to make his disciple's face shine like an angel, as did Stephen's. Christ is yet in the clouds of persecution to illuminate them for his people.

Christ came in the clouds of temptation. For forty days he was in the wilderness with the wild beasts, and was tempted of Satan. He was tempted in all points like as we are. He knew what it was to be hungry. He knew what it was to suffer from thirst. He knew what it was to be deserted by his friends. He knew what it was to be lied about and maligned. He knew what it was to have his most generous motives misunderstood. He knew what it was to be insulted, to be spit upon, crowned with thorns, and to go to the death. But in all these clouds of temptation there was no sin. Never once did he yield to the tempter. He made a pathway of light across all the clouds of temptation. He is still in the clouds of temptation with his people. No man need ever fear that there can gather around him temptations so dark that Christ will not be there to lighten the path and show him what he ought to do. And we have his promise that no man shall be tempted more than he is able to bear. Christ will be with us in every such cloud.

Christ came in the clouds of suffering. He wept tears at the grave of Lazarus. He spent a large part of his life in going where people were sick or in trouble, and his big heart overflowed in sympathy and love to everybody that was having a hard time. He went to the people that needed him most. He still comes in the clouds of sorrow. No one need ever sorrow without Christ for a companion. There need never be a sufferer unable to sleep in the dark night without having Christ with him in all the gentleness of his love, in all the tenderness of his sympathy, to sweeten the cup of sorrow by his presence.

Christ came in the clouds of toil and burden-bearing. He worked in the carpenter's shop during all his young manhood. He knows all about hard work. He took for his intimate friends fishermen and poor workingmen, who had to work hard to get a living. How he did brighten their lives for them! What marvelous compensation he gave for the old fishing-nets and boats they abandoned! Christ is still saying to men: "Come unto me, all ye that labor and are heavy-laden, and I will give you rest."

Christ came in the clouds of sin. Wherever the cloud gathered blackest, Christ came with tenderest mercy, to illuminate the clouds with forgiveness and hope. How black the sky around that poor wild man of the Gadarenes, who was "led captive by the devil at his will"! But Christ made all his sky bright again. How lowering and hopeless the clouds that hung over the head of that poor woman that was taken in sin, and was about to be stoned to death! But Christ's mercy dispersed her enemies, took the sting of guilt out of her own heart, and bade her hope again. We might multiply cases. I have in my house the copy of a painting called "The Rainmaker." It shows an Indian standing on the roof of a wigwam shooting his arrows into the clouds to cause rain. Christ is the sunshine-maker for this world. He can shoot his arrow into the blackest cloud of sin and cause it to dissolve in mercy and forgiveness, in sunshine and love, upon the head and heart of the poor sinner.

But he is coming again in other clouds. They are the clouds of judgment. Those who have met him in the clouds here, and have obeyed him and given him their hearts, will have no fear in meeting him in the clouds of judgment. If in the clouds of sin you have admitted him to your heart, and he has forgiven you and given you peace; if he has walked with you in the hours of trial and sorrow; if he has strengthened you in the hour of temptation,—then when he comes in the clouds of judgment you will mount up with him with infinite joy and gladness.

But some people who will see him coming in the clouds of judgment will be filled with consternation.

They will be those who have pierced his tender heart by the cruel spear of indifference or rejection; those to whom he has been kind and good, and yet they have denied him their confession, have refused him their friendship, have slighted him in the open congregation when his friends have spoken of his kindness and love and have made known their admiration and love for him. These have denied they ever knew him, by their silence and their refusal to confess him. He has come to them again and again, with the air of a suppliant, and begged of them to open their hearts to receive him as a guest. But they have closed the door in his face, and he has gone away grieved and pierced to the heart. They shall look on him whom they have pierced. In that hour they shall be among the number who will cry out for the rocks and for the mountains to fall upon them, and hide them from the face of him that sitteth on the throne.

Make sure of a happy meeting with Christ, then, by surrendering your heart to him now.

Some one says that there will be a password at the gate of heaven. Some will come up and knock repeatedly. The gatekeeper will say: "The password?" They will reply: "We have no password. We were great on earth, and now we come to be great in heaven." A voice from within will answer: "I never knew you."

Another group comes and knocks. The gatekeeper says: "The password?" They say: "We have no password. We have done many noble things on earth. We endowed colleges and gave large sums to charity." The voice from within again says: "I never knew you."

A third group approaches and knocks. The gatekeeper says: "The password?" The answer: "We were wanderers from God, and deserved to die; but we heard the voice of Jesus——"

"Aye, aye!" says the gatekeeper; "that is the password! Lift up your heads, ye everlasting gates, and let these people in!"

XXIII.

A CANDLESTICK IN DANGER.

But I have this against thee, that thou didst leave thy first love. Remember therefore from whence thou art fallen, and repent, and do the first works; or else I come to thee, and will move thy candlestick out of its place, except thou repent.—*Rev.* ii. 4, 5 (*Revised Version*).

THESE are words of warning and rebuke that were spoken by Christ to the church of Ephesus. This church had very much to be said in its favor. It was a splendid working church in many ways. It was famous for its work in the Lord's cause. It had a large number of people in it who patiently bore the burdens required to keep up in that place the preaching of the Gospel and the study of God's Word. It had a wide reputation as a thoroughly orthodox church; they were very careful, not only of the theology of their preachers, but of their members; and they are commended for this. The Savior declares that they have been a courageous church, and have not been of that sort of people who faint easily. I imagine there are a great many churches that would count it high honor to have these things said in their behalf. I think there are a good many churches who would think there was nothing left to be desired. But Jesus says there is a great deal lacking even after such a description. He declares that, in spite of their courage and their work and their patience, they are in danger of losing everything through a lack of that enthusiastic fervor and love which are dearer to his heart than anything else. The fact was that in the very midst of their working they had fallen away from the glow of love in which they rejoiced when they first gave their hearts to Christ. And Christ says by way of warning: "Remember therefore from whence thou art fallen, and repent, and do the first works; or else I come to thee, and will move thy candlestick out of its place, except thou repent."

Now, anything that is applicable to the church as a church is applicable to us as individuals. And while the church is represented as a great candlestick, the burning of whose candle makes a great light in the world, every man is intended to be a candle of the Lord, and Christ's ideal for every Christian is that he shall be the light of the world. Nothing can be more important than that every one of us shall be at our best in radiating influence for the advancement of Christ's kingdom among men, and we can not be at our best unless we are full of the fervor of love for Christ.

There used to be in Europe a famous swordsman named Scanderbeg, and on one occasion a great knight came a long distance to see the sword with which this swordsman had done such exploits. When it was shown to him, however, he was disappointed at the sight, and said that it looked to him like any other sword. The man who showed it to him replied, "You see the sword, but not the arm that wielded it." The sword of the Spirit, which is the Word of God, needs the arm of supreme love and devotion to wield it and make it irresistible.

This fervor of spirit which is dear to Christ is not something hard for us, but it is a thing that is natural to us, and it is therefore inexcusable for us to live without it when we have so great and heroic and loving a master to serve. I was reading this week of the heroism of some of our mothers in Revolutionary times. One of them, Mrs. Martin, was asked by a British officer whether she had a son.

"I have seven."

"Where are they?"

"Fighting for their country."

"All of them?"

"All."

The officer sneered. "Well, you sent enough," he said.

Mrs. Martin looked him squarely in the face, and said, "I wish I had fifty sons to send against you."

In these days, with a well-filled treasury and abundant resources, it is hard to understand how much woman's work counted in those early times. Mrs. Draper, of Dedham, Mass., not only sent her husband and her sixteen-year-old son to the army, but when they were gone she called in her neighbors and began baking bread and pies, which she kept on a long table before her gate for the refreshment of all hungry American soldiers who passed that way. After Bunker Hill, when the scarcity of ammunition induced Washington to call for all available pewter and lead, the same Mrs. Draper came to the front again. She had the finest collection of pewter dishes in all New England, a collection that would have been dear to the heart of any New England housekeeper. But without a moment's hesitation she put it in the fire and melted it down, and, not content with furnishing the material, obtained a mold and made the pewter into bullets and forwarded them to the army. Then a new want arose. The men were insufficiently clothed. The indefatigable Mrs. Draper had piles of domestic cloth stored away for family use. She made it into soldiers' coats. Her splendid stock of sheets and blankets was transformed into shirts, and much of her own flannel clothing was altered to men's garments.

That was the kind of fervor and love which was at the beginning of the American nation. Is it unnatural, then, that Jesus Christ should ask of us, in so holy a cause as the salvation of the world, that we shall not only give him service, but that we shall give him service that shall be irresistible because of the love and devotion that are in it?

Some people excuse themselves as they get older for this loss of fervor in their love and service for Christ. Some say that all love is in its very nature an illusion; that our enthusiasm for a person or for a cause is very largely a creation of our own fond imagination; and that the cold touch of reality slowly dispels that sort of thing. That is the doctrine of cynics. If we find that we have been deceived, and have loved one who was thought to be noble and good, but who afterward proved to be base and wicked, we can easily understand how love might die out from such a cause. But no man or woman in the history of this world ever lost their love for Jesus Christ in that way. Without any exception, the more people know of Christ the better they love him; the closer they come into touch with him, the better acquainted they get with him, the more enthusiastic is their love for him. There never has been an exception to that rule. You never yet heard a man say, no matter how far he had gone away from his Christian life, or how hard and wicked he had become,—you have never found one man that would tell you that when he was first introduced to Christ he was charmed with him and delighted, but that after he came to know him well and live in fellowship with him every day, he was disenchanted and lost his enthusiasm. No, men do not lose their love for

Christ in that way. It is when they wander away from Christ, and fail to keep up their friendship with him, that they forget how beautiful and glorious he is and come to lose their love for him.

Other people say that the emotions exhaust themselves, and that you can not expect people, as they get older, to have the same enthusiastic love for Christ as in their youth. What an absurd folly is that! Do not let the devil deceive you by any such false theory. Did you ever see a grandfather or grandmother whose love for grandchildren became exhausted because there were many of them? I think not. Love grows by what it feeds on. Your love has not exhausted itself because you loved Christ too much or served him too faithfully, but because you have starved your heart. There are no Christians in the world so happy as old Christians, those whose lives for half a century or more have had the background of a sweet love-story between their own hearts and Christ. This loving communion has grown sweeter to them through all the years.

Now, I know that, as I speak, the Holy Spirit is uncovering to some of you your own hearts, and you are asking yourselves what it is that has robbed you of the fervor of love which you knew when you first gave your heart to Christ. Perhaps some sin has come in and separated you from God. You are compromising with some sin which not only destroys your peace and joy as a Christian, but robs you of your influence. Dr. J. W. Chapman, of Philadelphia, tells this story, which came under his own observation: He had been preaching for several days in a city in Indiana. The people thronged the church, but the unsaved seemed to possess hearts of stone. Dr. Chapman could see no sign either of blessing or victory, and so one day he called the pastors together and requested them to release him from the engagement. When Dr. Chapman had ceased speaking, one minister said: "I know where the difficulty is, and I will try and correct it." And he did. One of the chief ushers in the meeting, a member of the church and a lawyer of high standing at the bar, was living a double life. His conduct was a reproof to the cause of Christ. Whenever he walked down the aisle, a spiritual chill swept over the audience. His pastor left the meeting of the ministers and went to this man's office, and when alone with him he said: "Judge, it is reported on the street that your life is not right, and that you are a hindrance in the prosecution of the efforts for a revival. If this is true, I want to help you, and if it is untrue I will be your friend." The old man's face became pale. "It is all true, and more, and I am the most miserable man in the world." They fell upon their knees, the arm of the minister about the judge; and when the prayer was ended he had the consciousness of God's forgiveness. At the next public service he was present. The sermon was ended, and Dr. Chapman's hands were raised to pronounce the benediction, when the old judge arose to say: "My friends, you have long known me as a professed Christian. I rise to say that I have dishonored my Lord and injured his cause. I ask your forgiveness, as I have asked and received his." The confession ended in sobs. There was no benediction; there was a baptism of tears; but that was the beginning of victory. The first invitation to the unsaved after that brought at least fifty to Christ, and ten days meant the salvation of hundreds.

I doubt not that some here need to hear that heart-searching story. You have driven away Christ by your sin. Cease to sin, and turn from it by repentance and faith, and he will come back to you again. Others of you have lost Christ and your love for him because you have ceased your Bible reading and your communion with him day by day in his Word and in prayer. You may find him again where you lost him.

There is an old story of a great king who married his daughter to a poor man who loved her; but his permission had a condition annexed to it—that whenever the man's side looked black, or whenever he lost his wedding ring, he should not only lose his wife, but lose his life also. One day, pursuing the chase, he fell into a quarrel, when he not only received a bruise on his left side, but lost his ring in the scuffle. The tumult over, he perceived the danger into which his own heedlessness had brought him, and, in bitterness of soul, shed many tears. In his sorrow he spied a book. Opening this, he found therein his ring, and the first words he read directed him to herbs of which a plaster applied would not fail to heal him. Thus he was cured, and his life and happiness were saved.

If some of you have bruised your heart with hatred and anger, or any sin, in the midst of the world's temptation; or if you have lost that wedding ring of love which was the pledge of your union with Jesus Christ your Savior, I know a Book where you may find that precious ring again, and a medicine for the cure of your bruised and sinful heart. Come back to the Book and the service of your Lord!

Some of you have lost your fervor because you have come to the city and, living in the midst of its temptations where you need church fellowship more than you ever did in your life, have neglected for months, and some of you for years, to unite yourself in close personal fellowship with God's people. When you had that fellowship you enjoyed the fervor of love; you lost it when you came away from that. Come back where you lost it, and you will find it again. In these great wicked cities Christ should have the open confession and service of every one that hopes in his name.

XXIV.

THE HIDDEN MANNA, THE WHITE STONE, AND THE NEW NAME.

To him that overcometh, to him will I give of the hidden manna, and I will give him a white stone, and upon the stone a new name written, which no one knoweth but he that receiveth it.—*Rev.* ii. 17 (*Revised Version*).

THIS Scripture is rich in beautiful promises that ought to charm and delight every soul. In Sabatier's "Life of St. Francis of Assisi" there is this sentence, "It is not easy to realize how many waiting souls there are in this world." When Jesus was here among men, everywhere he went he seemed to find somebody who was just waiting to receive the good he could do for him. He found many men and women with a bitter cry on their lips and a cruel agony in their hearts, who were waiting for some one to come and heal them or touch their souls with hope. It is that way yet; and happy the man or the woman who is given spiritual insight to behold the needs of those who are waiting for the Christ.

In the same book to which I have referred, there is also the statement that the human heart so naturally yearns to offer itself up that we have only to meet along our path some one who, doubting neither himself nor us, demands it without reserve, and we yield it to him at once. Natural religions fail because their founders have not had the courage to lay hold upon the hearts of men, consenting to no partition. Carlyle says, "Hero worship never dies, and can never die." Both of these great men are right. The human heart longs to surrender itself in love and worship to a worthy leader. Jesus Christ meets all these conditions. We do not need to exaggerate his personality by means of the imagination, for he is more perfect and splendid than the most brilliant imagination could conceive. He comes to us also in the consciousness of perfect power and wisdom and love, to lead us onward to triumph. Let us study for a few moments these three pictures which represent what Christ is waiting to do for us.

First, he wants to feed us on the only food that can give us perfect satisfaction and peace. How many there are who go hungry and starved, when they might feed at Christ's abundant table!

Rev. William Arnot says he was once the guest of a friend who had a favorite dog. The animal would come into the room where the family were sitting at the dinner table, and would stand looking at his master. If the master threw him a crumb, the dog would seize it before it got to the floor. But if he put a joint of meat down on the floor, the dog would look at it and leave it alone, as if it were too good for him. There are many people who go half-starved on crumbs which they pick up from the world's table, when God is offering them the whole joint.

A friend of mine was traveling in a train with a Christian business man, when the conversation turned on their personal experiences. The business man had been speaking about the troubles that had assailed him during the year, when suddenly he said: "Nevertheless, I have not had an anxious moment for ten years. I have had burdens grievous to bear, sorrows heavy and sore, difficulties numberless and vexatious, disappointments and embarrassments of various sorts; but none of these things have corroded my heart, nor have they distressed me with anxiety." Now here was a man who had not the first tinge of fanaticism about him, but is known as a level-headed business man, who lives in an atmosphere of spiritual peace because Christ his Savior feeds him on the hidden manna.

To you who are restless and uneasy, and are getting no sweet satisfaction out of life, I offer this hidden manna in Jesus Christ. The Christ who said to his disciples, "Peace I leave with you, my peace I give unto you: not as the world giveth give I unto you. Let not your heart be troubled, neither let it be afraid," can realize all that to-night for you.

But Christ offers to give you something else—

the White Stone. This was doubtless an allusion to an ancient mode of indicating approbation and acquittal. In Ovid you may find these lines

> "A custom of old, and still ordains,
> Which life or death by suffrage obtains;
> White stones and black within an urn are cast,—
> The first absolve, but death is in the last."

This ancient custom was something like our modern balloting, as is done in some secret orders by white and black balls. The white stone promised by our Lord is a full and complete justification in the Day of Judgment, through his righteousness. The Christian at the last great assize shall receive not the black stone of condemnation, but the white stone of salvation, through the merits of Him who died for sinners. But, thank God, we do not have to wait until the Judgment to have a glimpse of the white stone. God gives it to us here, in this world, when we, by his grace, overcome our sin.

Very beautiful and touching is the story of the conversion of Harriet Beecher Stowe, at the age of fourteen, as told in her "Life and Letters," recently published. Her father, Dr. Lyman Beecher, preached one morning on "Jesus as the Soul's Friend." After returning from the service, Harriet went to his study and threw herself into his arms, saying, "Father, I have given myself to Jesus." Looking down tenderly into his beloved child's face, the good man said, while he pressed her to his heart and his warm tears fell on her head:

"Is it so? Then has a new flower blossomed in the kingdom of heaven this day." And how that flower did blossom as the years passed on!

"I have given myself to Jesus," was the girl's shy way of describing the method by which she became a friend of the Savior, and received the white stone of love and forgiveness.

The white stone may also indicate our purity when we have yielded our hearts to the tender, loving touch of Christ. There is a story of a nun in an Italian convent, who once dreamed that an angel opened her spiritual eyes to see all men as they were. She looked upon so much wickedness that she shrank back in horror. But just then Christ appeared among them, with bleeding wounds, and the nun saw that whosoever pressed forward and touched the blood of Jesus at once became as white as snow. It is so in every-day life. Every day that men come to Christ in repentance and faith he cleanses them. Tho it be a poor drunkard, outcast from the plague of drink, the touch of Christ can purify his heart and hang about his neck the white stone of sobriety and honor.

This is a personal salvation. Upon the white stone is written our new name. When Jacob was returning from his long stay with Laban, and the rumor came that his wronged brother Esau was coming to get vengeance on him for the sin of his youth, Jacob in terror went out to spend the night in prayer. In that night of agony an angel came and wrestled with him through the hours, and at last Jacob conquered, and the angel said, "Thy name shall be no more Jacob, but Israel, for as a prince thou hast power with God and with man, and hast prevailed." And this new man, with a new name, became glorious in history. God wants to give you a new name to-night; the old name, that has been identified with sin and rebellion against God, is to be purged out, and the new name, which binds you to heaven and Christ, is to take its place.

There has recently died in Samoa a young girl of whom, in connection with the brilliant novelist, Robert Louis Stevenson, a delightful story is told. She was born on the 29th of February, and was grieving that she could not have a birthday as often as other little girls. Thereupon the kind story-writer agreed to give her his own birthday, and had a deed drawn up in full legal form, making the transfer. What was only a playful make-believe with the gentle-hearted story-teller is more than accomplished when Jesus Christ gives us the "new name" of kinship with himself.

Now all these glorious promises which Christ gives us are on the condition that we shall overcome our sins; and he offers to do that for us if we surrender ourselves to him; and he is able to make good his offer.

One night, in Chicago, a minister was making his way home when he saw a man leaning against a lamp-post. Stepping up to him and placing his hand on his shoulder, he inquired, "Are you a Christian?"

The man flew into a rage, doubled up his fist, and the preacher thought he was going to knock him into the gutter.

The minister said: "I am very sorry if I have offended you; but I thought I was asking a proper question."

"Mind your own business," he roared.

"That is my business," was the answer.

About three months later, on a bitter cold morning, about daybreak, some one knocked at the parsonage door.

"Who is there?" was asked.

A stranger answered, and the minister said, "What do you want?"

"I want to become a Christian," was the reply.

There isn't a parsonage door in the land that will not open at that cry; but the minister was astonished to see there the man who had cursed him for talking to him as he leaned against the lamp-post.

He said: "I am very sorry. I haven't had any peace since that night. Your words have haunted and troubled me. I could not sleep last night, and I thought I would come and get you to pray for me."

That man accepted Christ, and went away with the white stone and the new name written on it, and ever afterward fed on the hidden manna.

Now it all depends on you, whether you or the devil get the victory. Some of you who are here to-night were here last Sunday night. The Holy Spirit called to your conscience then. But you let the devil get the victory. You might have been feeding on hidden manna all this week, if you had not given way to the evil one and rejected Christ. Some of you have stayed away all the week because you were afraid that if you came to the week-night meetings you would be converted. How strange that a man should be afraid of getting rid of his sins, of finding forgiveness and peace and heaven! But you are here again to-night. God has mercifully granted you this new invitation. Who shall have the victory to-night—you or the devil? It is for you to decide, for if you resist the devil he will flee from you. You may go home with the assurance of victory in your heart; but your victory must come through surrender to Jesus Christ, the rightful Lord of your soul.

XXV.

THE SINNER'S OPEN DOOR.

Behold, I have set before thee a door opened, which none can shut.—*Rev.* iii. 8 (*Revised Version*).

EVERY man shall have a fair chance to be saved. The door of mercy is never locked against earnest souls. If you come with an honest heart to find out how to get freedom from your sins, seeking after peace with God, you will find no locks or bolts, but a door wide open. We used to sing an old song entitled "The Gates Ajar." But its teaching was misleading. The suggestion was that a man might barely squeeze through; that somehow God begrudged us the chance of salvation. But Jesus says that he has set before us a door opened, and no enemy of our souls, man, woman, or devil, has the power to shut it. Nothing can do that but our own wicked will.

In George Macdonald's novel, Robert Falconer, after feeding his soul on ashes until he was in despair, went to his box and took out the Bible that his mother had given him before he left home, and said, "Now I must find standing-ground." He proceeded to read over the life and words of Jesus, having all the time a little piece of paper by his side and a pencil in his hand, intending to write down the great foundation truths which he found there. These were the three which he wrote down: "First, that a man's business is to do the will of God; second, that God takes upon himself the care of the man; and third, therefore, that a man must never be afraid of anything." I wish you could all learn that lesson to-night. Christ has set before you an open door; if you will go straight through that door in obedience to him, he will take care of your future. And you may look up into his face and say, "O Lord, I have taken thee at thy word, I have obeyed thee, and I will trust thee and not be afraid."

Do not be afraid to enter that open door because of any consciousness of your own weakness or fear that you would not hold out as a Christian, for all you have to do is to stay inside the door; if you keep yourself in loving touch with Christ, he will grant you all the help you need for this new and divine life. Canon Wilberforce told Dr. Meyer that he once had his likeness painted by the great artist Herkomer, who told him this story. Herkomer was born in the Black Forest, his father being a simple wood-carver. When the artist rose to fame in London and had his luxurious studio, his first thought was to have the old father come and spend the rest of his years with him. He came, and was very fond of molding clay. All day he made things out of clay; but as the years passed he thought his hand would lose its cunning. He often went upstairs at night to his room with the sad heart of a man who thinks that his best days are gone by. Herkomer's quick eye of love detected this, and when his father was safe asleep his gifted son would come downstairs and take in hand the pieces of clay which his old father had left, with the evidences of defect and failure, and with his own skilful touch would make them as fair as they could be made by human hand. When the old man came down in the morning and took up the work he had left all spoiled the night before and held it up before the light, he would say, rubbing his hands with joy, "I can do it as well as ever I did."

Ah, is not that just what our Heavenly Father is wanting to do for you? How many marks of failure, how many scars of sin, how much that you are ashamed of has come into your life because you have disobeyed God and taken your life in your own hands—taken the bit between your own wilful teeth and refused to be guided by the Lord Jesus. But the Savior comes, with the marks of the thorns on his brow, with the nail-prints in his hands, and says: "Will you not yield to me? Behold, I have set before you a door opened; I will make your life pure and whole again; I will mold it into beauty again beyond your fondest dreams. Come through the door of mercy and be at peace."

Neither let any one refuse to enter this open door because there are things about it they can not understand and because the devil insinuates into your mind many doubts and fears. It does not make any difference how timidly or doubtingly a man gets through the door when he is invited to dinner—the dinner tastes just as good after he is once inside as if he had gone through the door with all the faith in the world and with all the boldness and assurance of an old friend.

Dr. Arthur Pierson tells the story of a minister who was in Scotland holding evangelistic services. He went around from house to house and talked with the villagers. Seeing an old lady sitting out on her balcony, he approached her and said, "My good woman, I suppose you are saved."

"Na," said she, "sir, I am na saved."

"Not saved," he said, "and brought up in old Scotland?"

"Na saved," she answered sadly.

"But," he said, "you understand the work of Jesus Christ, and you know that Jesus Christ died for you, don't you?"

"I kna that, but I'm na saved."

"And you know that salvation is dependent upon your acceptance of him, don't you?"

"Yes."

"Ah, then, why are you not saved?"

"Because my faith is na strong enough."

The minister answered: "It's not the strength of your faith; it is the strength of Jesus that saves you."

She could not see it. Over in the next field the evangelist saw a great bull grazing, and he called attention to the animal.

"Ah," said she, "he is a dreadful creature."

"But suppose he should charge on us?"

"May the Lord hae mercy on us!"

"Well, but," said he, "suppose you and I were in that field, and the mad creature should charge down on us?"

She was frightened at the very thought. He noticed, however, that there was a ravine in the field and over the deep ravine a stout plank. And he said: "Suppose the bull was chasing us and we came to that ravine, the vicious animal right behind, and I saw that the good old plank was going to sustain me, and passed safely over; but you come up and are very doubtful whether it will hold you up. But those cruel horns are behind, and you have got to go over. Now you get over as well as I, and the fact that you had little faith in the plank while I had much in it makes no difference in our salvation. Your little faith has carried you over the plank just as surely as my great faith carried me."

"I see," said she, "and the plank is Jesus!" And she found her way through the open door and was saved. Don't spend your time worrying about your weakness. Surrender your heart to Christ and depend upon his strength.

That door stands open for every poor sinner that will enter in. The condition of salvation is not the particular kind of sinner, but the size of the door; when a door stands open wide, it is not the kind of clothes a man has on that is important: it is whether the door is high enough and wide enough to let him in, and he is willing to go. The door is wide enough—"Whosoever will may come." The door is high enough—"Though your sins be as scarlet they shall be as white as snow; though they be red like crimson, they shall be as wool." It is all left with you. There is no greater folly than to grade your sins. Any sin is enough to ruin you. Come in through the open door of mercy, be born again into a new creature in Christ Jesus, and be adopted into the family of God.

A man once came, a poor wreck, full of despair, into a parsonage parlor. Drunkenness had dragged him down to a living hell. The minister told him the old story that is over new, that there was an open door before him, and that through God's mercy and Christ's redeeming love he might be born again, and become a partaker of the Divine nature, an heir of God and a joint heir of Jesus Christ. As a drowning man catches at a straw, he fell on his knees and cried: "My God! Can a dog like me become thy son?" He poured out his heart in tears and prayers, and rose up with transfigured face; and, with a new dignity that he had not known before, said: "I—I—am a child of God." The greatness of that sublime exaltation remained with him, and during all the rest of the years of his life the consciousness of his sonship to God was his safeguard and filled his life with sweetness and strength.

The door is open. No one can keep you out but yourself. It may be you will never go through the door; it is possible that you may miss heaven at last and be lost. But if you do it will be because, standing before the open door to-night, you trampled on your own conscience, grieved the Spirit of God, refused my pleading, and turned away and would not enter. Do not, I beg of you, commit such a folly. Outside is darkness and sin and death. Inside is forgiveness and peace and immortal glory.

XXVI.

THE CROWNED HEADS OF THE SPIRITUAL REALM.

Hold fast that which thou hast, that no one take thy crown.—*Rev.* iii. 11 (*Revised Version*).

A CROWN is the symbol of the summit of human power and glory. So true is this that, despite all our democratic training in this republic, there is scarcely anything in the Old World that is looked upon with more interest by American travelers than the famous crowns that have been worn by the emperors and czars and kings and queens of the historic past. The oldest crown in Europe is the "Iron Crown" of Lombardy. It is resting now in the cathedral of Monza, in a little town upon the mountain-side above Milan. For thirteen hundred years it has held its place as the most famous European crown. The last man who wore it was that giant robber, the first Napoleon. In May, 1805, he assembled at Milan a great royal and military assemblage, and in their presence he placed this famous old Iron Crown upon his head, repeating the proud motto which goes with it, "God has given it to me; wo to him who touches it." But the Iron Crown went down, nevertheless, before the soldiers of the Iron Duke. In the regalia-room of the Scottish kings in Edinburgh Castle one can still see among other valuable relics the coronation crown of that romantic hero, Robert Bruce. This crown was made out of the gold ear-rings and chains of the high-born ladies of Scotland, contributed for that purpose by these loyal women when Robert Bruce was an outlaw, before he won his kingdom. In the ancient cathedral of Aix-la-Chapelle, in Aachen, Germany, there is a crown of great historic interest which has been preserved there for more than a thousand years. It was worn by the great Charlemagne, whose tomb is not far distant. This crown has been placed, since he wore it, on the heads of thirty emperors, each one wearing it his little day of trial and trouble, of victory and defeat, and then passing it on to somebody else to worry over in his turn. It has not now been used for nearly a hundred years. There are several of the crowns of the French kings preserved in the Louvre, in Paris, one of them going back to the time of the long-haired chieftains who flourished about the beginning of the seventh century. The new crown of Queen Victoria has its entire surface completely covered with jewels, many of which are famous in history. There is one heart-shaped ruby, said to have been worn by Edward the Black Prince. The estimated value of the crown is five million dollars.

But, after all, the most famous crown this world has ever seen was a crown made of thorns. It was platted by Roman soldiers and placed on the brow of Jesus of Nazareth more than eighteen hundred years ago. Multitudes of people who never heard of these famous historic crowns which I have mentioned have wept tears of sympathy and love for him who wore that crown of thorns, and have crowned him in their hearts King over all. He does not wear the crown of thorns now, but a crown of glory. All the crowns are to become his. John, in his vision on the Isle of Patmos, saw the Savior, "and on his head were many crowns." Putting the crowns on the head of Christ means the coming of universal love and peace. There is not a crown in the museums of the Old World that does not suggest bloodshed and carnage. The history of the world has been written in blood by the bitter struggles of ambitious men and women seeking for an earthly crown. But the crowning of Christ means peace on earth and good-will to men.

The Scripture we are studying is a personal appeal to each one of us to do our own part and share in the glory of the triumph of Jesus Christ, not only in this world, but in that immortal realm to which we are hastening. "Hold fast that which thou hast," says our Master, "that no one take thy crown."

Let us reflect on some of the crowns which are within our reach. Paul, in his second letter to

Timothy, when he had come to be an old man, says: "I am now ready to be offered, and the time of my departure is at hand. I have fought a good fight, I have finished my course, I have kept the faith: henceforth there is laid up for me a crown of righteousness, which the Lord, the righteous judge, shall give me at that day: and not to me only, but unto all them also that love his appearing." What a joyous outlook was that!—"a crown of righteousness." Righteousness is always a symbol of dignity and honor, while sin is forever a brand of dishonor and shame. The Savior must have had in his mind this thought concerning the supreme dignity and value of righteousness when he said: "Seek ye first the kingdom of God, and his righteousness, and all these things [referring to temporal necessities] shall be added unto you." The man who is right, whose heart and conduct are pure, and who is conscious that there is no stain upon him, stands before a righteous court wearing a crown of righteousness with calmness and dignity. He can afford to be calm. One can conceive, of course, of a court being corrupt and wicked, or of the evidence being bribed and perjured, and a righteous man coming to grief in such a court. But you and I are to stand before a court where there will be no bribing, and where there will be no dispute about the evidence. If the righteous Judge in that court shall place the crown of righteousness on our heads, there will not be one soul in the universe to dispute our right to it. But one can not wear the badge of sin here and the crown of righteousness there. We must begin to be clothed upon with that righteous life here and now. We must carry the dignity and joy of the Savior's righteousness with us from the earth up to the judgment-seat. What we are when we leave the earth, that we shall be when we arrive there. If we wear a crown of righteousness in heaven we must begin to wear it here on earth. If any that hear me are conscious that they are uncrowned, listen to the invitation of heaven: "Come now, and let us reason together, saith the Lord: though your sins be as scarlet, they shall be as white as snow; though they be red like crimson, they shall be as wool." And note how Paul, who came to the end of his life with such a glorious prospect before him, obtained his crown. In his first letter to Timothy he says: "This is a faithful saying, and worthy of all acceptation, that Christ Jesus came into the world to save sinners; of whom I am chief." The crown of righteousness is within the reach of every one who will accept salvation in the name of Jesus.

The Apostle James tells us of another crown. "Blessed is the man," he says, "that endureth temptation: for when he is tried, he shall receive the crown of life, which the Lord hath promised to them that love him." Don't forget that in the hour of temptation. It is not for nothing that the

Christian endures temptation and denies himself for Christ's sake; there is a crown of immortality at stake. Everything grows old here and soon shows the marks of age and decay; but the Christian is hastening toward a land where he shall wear the crown of eternal life; a land where there shall be no more hunger or thirst; a realm where there shall be no more severe changes of climate to test the constitution; a land that shall need neither the light of the sun nor of the moon; a land where there shall be no sorrow, and where aching hearts and tears shall be unknown; a glorious realm where every citizen shall wear a crown—a crown of life. Bonar, the hymn-writer, describes that land as a place—

> "Where the faded flower shall freshen—
>   Freshen nevermore to fade;
> Where the shaded sky shall brighten—
>   Brighten nevermore to shade.
>   .   .   .   .   .
>
> Where the bond is never severed;
>   Partings, claspings, sob, and moan,
> Midnight waking, twilight weeping,
>   Heavy noontide—all are done.
> Where the child has found its mother;
>   Where the mother finds the child;
> Where dear families are gathered
>   That were scattered on the wild;
> Where the hidden wound is healed;
>   Where the blighted life reblooms;
> Where the smitten heart the freshness
>   Of its buoyant youth resumes;

> Where we find the joy of loving
>   As we never loved before—
> Loving on, unchilled, unhindered,
>   Loving once forevermore."

Peter has still another crown which he sets before us. He says that, if we are faithful, "When the chief Shepherd shall appear we shall receive a crown of glory that fadeth not away." That is something which can not be said of any earthly crown. While it may outlast the man for whom it was made, his power to hold the crown soon passes by, and it falls from his trembling brow. Many times earthly monarchs have found that the trouble and sorrow and anxiety that came with the crown robbed it of all its value, and long before they have yielded it up to the demand of death its glory has faded away for them. But to the Christian there is promised a crown of glory which shall never fade away. Our glory is to be the glory of our Master. Christ, in that wonderful prayer for his disciples and for all those who should believe on him through their word, unto the end of time, which is recorded in the seventeenth chapter of St. John's Gospel, utters these words: "The glory which thou gavest me I have given them; that they may be one, even as we are one: I in them and thou in me, that they may be made perfect in one; and that the world may know that thou hast sent me, and hast loved them, as thou hast loved me. Father, I will that they also, whom thou hast given me, be with me where I am; that they may behold my glory which thou hast given me." Our glory is to be the glory of sharing with Jesus Christ in blessing the world while we are in it, and sharing his glorious life and work through all eternity in heaven.

How the devil does lie to people and cheat them, when he allures them by worldly glitter and tinsel away from the true glory one may have as a fellow-heir with Jesus Christ! As Dr. Henson says, the devil makes people think if they enter upon a religious life they will be placed in a sort of ecclesiastical garden where they will not dare to touch anything, and where the sign "Keep off the Grass" will be everywhere. There could not be a more false idea of the joy and glory of fellowship with Christ.

There is still another crown possible for us. In his first letter to the Thessalonians Paul says: "For what is our hope, or joy, or crown of rejoicing? Are not even ye in the presence of our Lord Jesus Christ at his coming? For ye are our glory and joy." To every one, then, who shall lead another to Christ there shall be a special crown of rejoicing. Dr. Watkinson, of London, tells about a very poor but good woman who had led her children to Christ, who, when she died, was carried to the grave from a lowly cottage. But her children in grateful remembrance and with prophetic hope and confidence put this verse on her funeral card: "And a great sign was seen in heaven; a woman arrayed with the sun, and the moon under her feet, and upon her head a crown of twelve stars." And those children were right. A good woman who by her prayer and faith and self-denying love wins her children to God and brings them up in loving fellowship with Christ, sending them out into the world to be witnesses for him, is great enough to have the sun for a robe, the moon for a footstool, and the most glorious planets for the stars of her forehead. What about your crown of rejoicing? Are you gathering any stars that will shine in radiant joy in your crown?

Let me lay the emphasis a moment upon the individuality of all these crowns: "Hold fast that which thou hast, that no one take thy crown." This is a personal matter. You personally and individually are here in the midst of all these tides and currents which make up what we call human life. What can you and what will you do with these privileges and opportunities which are within your reach? The power is yours. God has given you a will by which you can choose and decide. You can use all these powers within your grasp selfishly, for your own interest, if you choose to do so. On the other hand, you may submit them to the will of Christ and use them righteously and generously, so that they shall win for you a crown of righteousness and glory that fadeth not away. But remember this, that the duty which belongs to you can never be shifted off on to anybody else.

There are personal duties and obligations which grow out of the fact that they appeal to your own personality and to nobody else. In time of war, where there is a draft to obtain soldiers, rich men often hire substitutes to fight in their places; but this is a case where a substitute will not answer. Alone and individually you must answer to God for the gifts and opportunities which he has placed within your reach. If you are ever crowned in heaven, it will be because you sought the crown earnestly and personally, with a sincere and faithful heart. And our Scripture suggests that it is possible for us to lose the crown that by nature belongs to us.

A drunken man met another man perfectly sober, but very worldly, in a business man's office. They had been intimately acquainted in other years, during which time both had been Christian workers. The younger man had once meant to devote himself to the ministry, but had become worldly and was now practically out of the church, altho having no specially vicious habits. It was evident that he had lost his friendship for his former comrade, and by his cold and haughty manner he endeavored to repel him. The half-drunken man was a keen observer and a good judge of human nature. He saw that he was annoying the other man, and the spirit of mischief led him on. Finally he referred to their former experiences as workers in the church; recalled certain incidents in which they had shared; spoke of the gradual growth of their coldness and indifference, and concluded by exclaiming in a really earnest and heart-rending manner: "God help us, John; you and I have lost our way to the throne!" Both of these men had cast away their crowns—the worldly man just as surely as the poor drunkard. They had lost the crown through unfaithfulness.

Do I speak to any to-night who are losing their way to the throne in the same manner? The way to the throne is marked by prayerfulness, earnest study of God's Word, a constant watchfulness to know the will of Christ, seeking daily to please him and share with him in the salvation of the lost. "Hold fast that which thou hast, that no one take thy crown."

XXVII.

A PILLAR IN THE TEMPLE.

He that overcometh, I will make him a pillar in the temple of my God, and he shall go out thence no more: and I will write upon him the name of my God, and the name of the city of my God, the new Jerusalem, which cometh down out of heaven from my God, and mine own new name.—*Rev.* iii. 12 (*Revised Version*).

There is in the Bible no picture more comforting than this used to encourage a man or a woman to press forward in the face of every obstacle and give the heart unreservedly to do the will of God. There is no more serviceable or noble part of the temple than the pillars. It is always noble to be serviceable. What a wonderful revelation it is of Christ's heart, when he offers to take poor sinners —who have grieved him, and rebelled against him, and it may be have brought his name into evil repute—and if by his grace they will repent of their sins and confess them, he will not only forgive them, but trust them and honor them by making them living pillars in his temple!

How much more splendid is the forgiveness of God than that which is commonly called forgiveness among men! A merchant sometimes forgives the employee who has sinned against him; but he will not put him in any place of trust again. A man said to me not long ago, about one of his employees, that there was a time that he would have trusted that man with anything, and he was glad to help him along; but the man deceived him and betrayed the trust. His first thought was to throw him out entirely and publicly disgrace him and prosecute him before the court; but he had pity for the man's family, and because the man seemed repentant for his sin and begged for a new chance of life he kept him in his employment. But he said to me, "I will never trust him again where he has any chance to deceive me about money."

He had forgiven him; he had no anger, no prejudice, against him; he wished him no harm,—but he could not trust him. But how marvelous in contrast with this is the forgiveness of Christ! He takes those who have betrayed him, who have crucified him afresh by their sinfulness and put his name to an open shame, and when they repent and turn to him in faith, he not only forgives them, but makes them pillars in his temple.

There is nothing more wonderful than the way Christ has taken poor sinners, who had no name except one to be sneered at, and when they have given themselves up to him to do his will, has not only saved, but honored, them, so that their names stand through the centuries as pillars in the temple of the Lord. There was that poor, drunken, blaspheming tinker in the Bedford jail in England, whom everybody despised until he surrendered his heart to Christ; and the Savior transformed him into one of the noblest names in human history. Not a nobleman in the land but looked down on him while he was on earth; yet a while ago, when a monument was unveiled to him, a duke was proud to preside at the ceremony; and there is probably not a duke in England, good or bad, who would not be glad to pay honor to John Bunyan. And God is no respecter of persons. He is as ready and willing to honor any one here, however frail and sinful, if you will repent, as he was to honor John Bunyan.

Nothing is more marvelous than the kind of material God can use, and by his infinite skill and love make something splendid and heavenly out of it. There was once in the Carmelite monastery in Paris a cook who was called Brother Lawrence. He was led to give himself to Christ, and with holy longing he opened his heart in prayer for goodness. At first he was so ignorant he could not even read his Bible, but he became so good and noble a man that people wrote to him from all over the world of his day, asking the secret of his holiness. Some of his letters have come down to us, and the whole secret of his life was simply this: that he got the conception of thinking of God's love for him; and when he picked up a straw from the kitchen floor, he did it because God loved him; and when he watched the buds and the leaves come out on the trees in the spring, he drew therefrom the thought that God was loving him; and all that he did he did, not because he loved God, but because God loved him. He had come into fellowship with John when he says: "Herein is love, not that we love God, but that he loved us." His life was illuminated and glorified by this appreciation of the love of God for him. Sydney Lanier most beautifully sings of the possibility of entrenching ourselves in this consciousness of God's greatness and love for us:

> "As the marsh-hen secretly builds on the watery sod,
>   Behold, I will build me a nest on the greatness of God;
>   I will fly in the greatness of God as the marsh-hen flies
>   In the freedom that fills all the space 'twixt the marsh and
>   the skies;
>   By so many roots as the marsh grass sends in the sod,
>   I will heartily lay me a-hold on the greatness of God."

This little song ought to set very clearly before your thoughts the fact that your salvation does not depend on your own strength, but on God's strength. You are to be a pillar in the temple of God not because of your goodness, but because the righteousness of Jesus Christ abides in your heart and his love dwells in you and strengthens you day by day.

I want to impress upon your heart that it is not only in heaven at last that the Lord will make you a pillar, but he will make you a pillar, honorable, happy, and glad, here and now. Dr. Wharton says that there are some people like the old monks who went about with a woful air, and when they met they would say: "Brother, we must die." Then the other would say, "Yes, we must die," until people would feel like saying: "Go on and die, both of you." Thank God, the Christian religion does not wait to begin its joy until we are dead. It begins the moment we come through the open door of mercy into God's temple and give ourselves up to be used and honored of him. Things here present are ours, as well as the things to come. The devil is false and deceives you when he makes you think you will have a happier life by staying out of the church and serving him instead of Christ. Billy Bray, an eccentric character over in England, was digging potatoes in his garden, and the potatoes were not turning out very well. The season had been bad for them, and they were of rather a poor quality. And so the devil insinuated into Billy's mind: "Billy, your Father doesn't love you very much, or he would give you better potatoes than those." But Billy was a true Christian and pulled himself together and said to Satan: "Who are you? Why, you haven't got a 'tater-skin in the world to bless yourself with, and what right have you to come insulting my Father?" When you resist the devil like that, you will get the best of him every time.

Alexander the Great came to visit Diogenes, the philosopher, who dwelt in a tub. When Alexander came to him and stood in the entrance to the little hovel in which he lived, and asked, in a patronizing way, "Diogenes, is there anything which Alexander the king can do for you?" the old philosopher replied: "Yes, there is one thing you can do for me—stand out of my sunlight." The only conversation that you and I need to have with the devil is to order him out of our sunlight. Some of you ought to do that to-night. He stands between you and the Sun of Righteousness. Order him out of the way. Enter the open door of the temple that God has set before you.

Not one of you here can dream of how much beauty and honor Christ will bring into your life if you will just give yourself entirely up to him. Surrender yourself to be just what he wants you to be. As Dr. Judson walked the streets of a heathen city men would ask: "Who is that going along there?" And the men who knew him would answer: "That is Jesus Christ's man." He had so identified himself with Jesus Christ in that heathen community that when they saw him they saw Christ. In the biography of Dr. Gordon, the great Boston preacher who went to heaven a few years ago, the story is told that he sat talking one day with a member of his church, and a little child sat listening, watching the holy glow on his face, and feeling impressed with the spiritual atmosphere of that good man. When he went away, the child looked into his mother's face and said: "Mother, was that Jesus?"

It is these divine possibilities that I offer you to-night. It is not to a poor, beggarly existence I am calling you; but to the richest and most glorious life that was ever lived in the world. And it is for the very frailest and most sinful one here, if you will only surrender your heart entirely to the indwelling of Christ. Let Christ dwell in you, then you shall dwell, a living, helpful, noble pillar, in his temple. He will put his new name upon you. I don't know what his new name is, but, please God, I intend to know. What glorious names we have already for him! But in the triumph that is coming to us after a while in heaven, some new name for our Savior, sweeter and more precious than any the world knows now, shall be inscribed on us, to our glory.

And let me ring the changes on the truth that the sweetest, the happiest, the most perfect Christian life that ever was lived may be lived by you, and that there never was a holier man or woman than God's grace in Jesus Christ can make of you. I could not offer you that divine equality in many things. Some of you never can make as much money as some other people. Some of you will never make as good a speech as some one else. But in that supreme life of heart fellowship with God, which makes the soul a pillar in the living temple of the Lord, there is nobody that may be more splendid than you. How well James Russell Lowell expresses the truth that the best things are easier to get than the poorest; that the heart of God is an open door:

> "At the devil's booth all things are sold,
>   Each ounce of dross costs its ounce of gold;
>   For a cap and bells our lives we pay,
>   Bubbles we buy with a whole soul's tasking:
>   'Tis heaven alone that is given away,
>   'Tis only God may be had for the asking."

XXVIII.

THE POOREST PEOPLE IN THE WORLD.

Because thou sayest, I am rich, and have gotten riches, and have need of nothing; and knowest not that thou art the wretched one and miserable and poor and blind and naked: I counsel thee to buy of me gold refined by fire, that thou mayest become rich; and white garments, that thou mayest clothe thyself, and that the shame of thy nakedness be not made manifest; and eyesalve to anoint thine eyes, that thou mayest see.—Rev. iii. 17, 18 (Revised Version).

THERE are many people who are following in the wake of the Pharisees in our day. They think they have somehow gotten together a good deal of moral and spiritual wealth on their own account; when, as a matter of fact, they have lived here in the midst of Christian influences, and have associated with Christian people in such a way that, almost in spite of themselves, they have received through God's mercy many admirable moral qualities, for which they have never given him any thanks. It is as if a man might go to the diamond fields in Africa and stroll around over the territory of a great mining company and pick up precious gems for which he never gave any thanks or made any return to the company about whose rich mine he found his jewels. This world is honeycombed with veins of precious gems of Christ's influence, and many a man has been so enriched in his nature by the prayers of his Christian mother, by the influence of the Christian education he received, by the Bible he learned in the Sunday-school, that it has hedged him away from disgraceful sins into which he would have fallen, and he imagines that it is his goodness; and so he is rather proud of himself. God says that such a man is very poor, is in great danger, and is to be pitied.

Mark Guy Pearse tells a very pretty little fable about a brier which was growing in a ditch, and there came along a gardener with his spade. As he dug around it and lifted it out the brier said to itself: "What is he doing that for? Doesn't he know that I am an old worthless brier?" But the gardener took it into the garden and planted it amid his flowers, while the brier said: "What a mistake he has made—planting an old brier like myself among such rose-trees as these!"

But the gardener came once more, and with his keen-edged knife made a slit in the brier, and "budded" it with a rose, and by and by, when summer came, lovely roses were blooming on that old brier.

Then the gardener said: "Your beauty is not due to that which came out of you, but to that which I put into you."

No man here has any reason to be proud of his

spiritual achievements, tho God has brought out of some, who were at one time but dry sticks, some very beautiful roses. And he wants to do that with every one of us. What a wonderful promise that is in Isaiah: "Instead of the thorn shall come up the fir tree, and instead of the brier shall come up the myrtle tree." God wants to take away all your thorns and give you instead abundant fruitfulness. Are you not willing to let the thorns go that you may have the flowers and the perfume? God knows that I want to get rid of my thorns, and I feel that in my heart of hearts I am willing to exchange them for God's roses. Shall we not all do that with one accord to-night?

Our text teaches us that there can be no sadder thing than to be deceived about ourselves—to always be seeing the faults of other people, the mote that is in our brother's eye, but failing to understand that the beam that is in our own eye makes it impossible for us to rid our brother of his infirmity.

A lady once went to Mr. Moody and said: "You made me perfectly wretched yesterday when you were preaching."

"How was that?" he asked.

"Well," she answered, "you said you pitied a man or woman who had never had the luxury of leading a person into the light. I don't know that I ever led any one to Christ. When I was married, I thought that my husband was near the kingdom of God, and that I was going to have no trouble in leading him into it."

"Well, what is the trouble now?" Mr. Moody asked.

"I don't know," she said, "but I can not talk to him as I once could. My words seem cold and empty, and he does not seem to like to have me speak to him on religious subjects. I wish you would pray for my husband."

"Now," said the minister, "let me ask you a few questions. Do you ever get out of temper with your husband and give him a good blowing up?"

"Yes, I do."

"Then, when you want to talk to him, you have a sort of feeling that you are not all right yourself."

"That is it exactly."

"Then you have trouble with the servants. If they burn the food, you go into the kitchen and make the air around blue; and when you want to talk seriously to your servants, your words seem to have no effect."

"Yes, that is true."

"Now," said Moody, "instead of praying for your husband, hadn't I better pray for you?"

The woman was humble and penitent enough now, and said: "I wish you would." They had prayer, and she went home.

Ten days later she came back and said: "Mr. Moody, if I had known you were going to talk to me in the way you did, I would never have come near you. I never saw myself as I did that day. I saw how unlike Jesus Christ I had been; how I had grown irritable; how I had lacked patience. I saw, for the first time in my life, that my husband was stumbling over me. I saw, if I was ever going to get right, I must make confession; so when my husband came home that night, I met him in the hall, threw my arms around his neck, and asked him to forgive me. 'Forgive you?' he said. 'For what?' 'I have been a Christian a great many years,' I said, 'and yet I have often been out of temper with you and I have spoken hasty, unkind words, and I am afraid that you are stumbling over me; and God knows that I love your soul more than anything on earth.' And do you know, my husband broke down then and there, and said he wished he was a Christian, and before the next morning God gave me my husband. I was so blessed that I called my servants together and confessed to them how irritable I had been; and, if you will believe it, my servants all broke down and said that they wanted to know how to become Christians, and three of them have been converted. I have had a large Bible class, but I do not think any of them have been converted; I have accomplished more during the last ten days than in all my former Christian life put together."

You see, so long as this woman was satisfied with herself, and thought she was spiritually rich, she was really poor and impoverished and worse than bankrupt in Christian influence. But when she saw the real state of the case, and recognized her own poverty, God made her rich in spiritual gold and gave her marvelous influence in winning souls.

The thing that is on my heart tonight more than anything else is to arouse in myself, as well as in you, a keen perception of how utterly dependent we are on God, and what folly it is for us to think that we are able to take care of ourselves, and can afford to be careless and indifferent concerning the commandments of him in whose hands is our very breath. The strongest man here physically may die in an hour, in spite of anything on earth he can do to prevent it. The richest person in the city has not wealth enough to ward off the common dangers of life. After all our shrewdness and all our wisdom and all our precautions, our life is yet in the hand of God, and we have no strength and no wealth which is independent of him—nothing except what he grants us from hour to hour.

Two Americans who were crossing the Atlantic met on Sunday night in the steamer cabin to sing hymns. As they sang Charles Wesley's greatest hymn, "Jesus, Lover of my Soul," one of the Americans heard an unusually rich and beautiful voice behind him. He looked around, and altho he did not know the face, he thought he recognized the voice. So when the music ceased he turned and asked the man if he had not been in the Civil

War. The man replied that he had been a Confederate soldier.

"Were you at such a place on such a night?" asked the first.

"Yes," he said, "and a curious thing happened that night; this hymn recalled it to my mind. I was on sentry duty on the edge of a wood. It was a dark night and very cold, and I was a little frightened because the enemy was supposed to be close at hand. I felt homesick and miserable, and about midnight, when everything was still, I was beginning to feel very weary, and thought that I would comfort myself by praying and singing a hymn. I remember singing this hymn:

> "'All my trust on thee is stayed,
> All my help from thee I bring;
> Cover my defenseless head
> With the shadow of thy wing.'

After I had sung those words a strange peace came down upon me, and through the long night I remember having felt no more fear."

"Now," said the other man, with tears in his eyes and in his voice, that added great effectiveness to his speech, "listen to my story. I was a Union soldier, and was in the wood that night with a party of scouts. I saw you standing up, altho I did not see your face, and my men had their rifles focused upon you, waiting the word to fire; but when you sang out,—

> " ' Cover my defenseless head
> With the shadow of thy wing,'

I said: 'Boys, put down your rifles; we will go home.' I could not kill you after that."

You see, our life is in God's hand; not only our physical existence, but all that is dear to us. We must trust him; we are poor and frail and useless unless God puts his arm about us and makes us rich and strong and beautiful as his children. Thank God, his gold is for sale to-night on such terms that every one of you can buy in abundance. What he asks is a surrender of yourselves. "Son, give me thy heart," is ever his appeal. That is always the appeal of a father to a son, and God is our Heavenly Father. Our self-righteousness is only as filthy rags in his sight, but our love, our obedience, our confession of him—that is priceless in his eyes, and he will pay us heaven's gold for that. The time is coming when one ounce of that gold will outweigh all the wealth of this world in your eyes; to-night you may have it in abundance. Come, and let God enrich your soul!

XXIX.

CHRIST KNOCKING AT THE HEART'S DOOR.

Behold, I stand at the door and knock: if any man will hear my voice and open the door, I will come in to him, and will sup with him, and he with me.—*Rev.* iii. 20 (*Revised Version*).

ONE of the sweetest promises which Christ makes to us is that, in our dealings with God, if we knock, it shall be opened to us; we shall never find the watchman asleep inside of mercy's door. We shall never find the gate-keeper a sluggard about opening the door to us when we knock to be let in to heaven's kindness and forgiveness. How strange it should be different on the other side when Christ comes knocking at the door of our hearts! How gracious beyond all comparison it is that he should come at all! But in his great love, when our ignorance and sin keep us from going to knock at the door of mercy, he comes as a suppliant to our door and knocks there for admission.

You have all, no doubt, seen copies of that great picture painted by Holman Hunt which he has called "The Light of the World." It represents a door that has been closed so long that the ivy has grown over it. The Christ whom he has painted standing on the doorstep has a face infinitely patient and benevolent. He is dressed like a priest, and he carries in his hand the lamp of truth. He has the attitude as he stands of one who has knocked again and again; but the eye beaming with love and the face that glows with yearning show the purpose to wait and not go away unless compelled. There is no latch outside the door, which rightly interprets the Scripture teaching that the lock of our hearts is on the inside, and that we must open the door if the Savior ever finds his way into our hearts.

The artist Bida has painted another picture—of the five foolish virgins who had neglected to take oil in their lamps—which would make a very suggestive companion-piece to Holman Hunt's great work. In Bida's picture the virgins have gone into the town to buy oil, and have returned to find that in their absence the wedding guests have gone, and they have knocked and knocked and have been refused admission. In their despair they have thrown themselves down on the steps of the palace in an attitude of hopeless sorrow. In one of these pictures you see the Savior waiting at the heart's door, knocking for admission, and in the other you see the sorrow of those who have refused to admit him, but who have been at last, too late, aroused to see their folly. How tenderly and with what insight into the heart Tennyson has interpreted the sorrow of that hour:

> "Late, late, so late! And dark the night, and chill!
> Late, late, so late! But we can enter still.
>   'Too late, too late! Ye can not enter now.'
>
> "No light! so late! and dark and chill the night—
> O let us in, that we may find the light.
>   'Too late, too late! ye can not enter now!'
>
> "Have we not heard the Bridegroom is so sweet!
> O let us in, tho late, to kiss his feet.
> O let us in, O let us in,
> O let us in, tho late, to kiss his feet.
>   'No! no! too late! ye can not enter now!'"

God forbid that any one of us, at whose heart's door the Christ has knocked with such tenderness so long, should ever take part in a hopeless scene like that!

How clearly this picture impresses upon us the divine character of our Lord. No mere man that ever lived could have used such a figure as that. Imagine Shakespeare, or Napoleon, or Frederick the Great, or Gladstone, using a figure like that! It is absurd. The whole presentation of Jesus Christ to us in the Bible pictures him to us as divine. He took upon himself our human nature in order to our salvation; but in the life of Jesus there is not one single instance recorded that reveals his manhood to us, that does not in the same incident reveal him to us as God.

Dr. Alexander McKenzie says that in his younger day he sought for a new way of teaching the doctrine of Christ. He was giving lectures to students, and he told them to get a sheet of paper and divide it into three columns. In the first column they were to write every passage where Christ was spoken of as God-man, in the second column all the passages where Christ was spoken of as God alone, and in the third all the passages where he was spoken of as man alone. The first column and the second filled right up, but the third column never got a single entry. He never found a passage speaking of Christ as man alone. At first glance some of you will think that that can not be; but if you will investigate, you will find it to be absolutely correct. There is one place where we read that Jesus went to sleep in a boat. That surely is like a man. But read the passage through. Jesus was asleep in the boat; his frightened disciples awoke him, and he rose up and said to the winds and waves: "Peace, be still!" That was the work of God. One day he had been traveling on foot for many miles and was tired out. He sat down beside a well to rest while his disciples went into a nearby town to buy food. A woman came up with a water-bottle on her head, and he said: "Won't you be kind enough to give me a drink of water?" Certainly that was just like a man. But after they had had a very interesting conversation together, he said: "Woman, he that drinketh of this water shall thirst again; but he that drinketh of the water that I shall give him shall never thirst; but the water that I shall give him shall be in him a well of water, springing up into everlasting life." That was the language of God.

But, you say, there was his death on the cross. A helpless man nailed to the wood. The head falling upon the breast, the dying groans, the blood dropping from the hands and feet, and the brow torn with thorns; the soldier thrusting the spear into his side, while the victim bows his head and dies. But that is only part of the story. While he was dying there upon the cross a poor sinner, full of remorse and with a glimmer of belief that this man by his side was something more than man, cries out in his heartbreak: "Lord, remember me when thou comest into thy kingdom!" And Christ, forgetting his own agony, answered with the assuring voice of Almighty God: "This day shalt thou be with me in Paradise." He did not point the dying man away from himself. He died; but the hands outstretched upon the cross opened the gate of Paradise for a dying sinner.

It is this Divine Christ who is knocking at the door of your hearts. It is not a weak man like yourself, but it is the loving Savior, who came down from the skies, who is able to come into your hearts and, dwelling there, cast out every evil guest and give you strength in every time of weakness and temptation. Your sins overcome you now because you are the passive victim of them, or because you yield yourself to them. Admit Christ into your heart, and you at once become aggressive in fighting them. And the moment you enter into fellowship with Christ and resist the devil he will flee from you.

A young man tells how he became a Christian while he was in college. It was during his absence from the school. When he came back, the men used to gather around the open fire in the room of one of the young men in his class. One evening some one started a smutty story. This young fellow, who had given his heart to Christ, quietly got up and went out. Next evening they gathered again, and some one cracked a smutty joke. He got up and went out. The third time when it happened somebody said: "What is the matter with you, Jim?" "Well," said he, "I can't stand that sort of thing. It is bad for me, and it is bad for all of us. It is unmanly and un-Christian, and I am going to get out." A very silly, insignificant young fellow in the party said: "Jim has got pious!" Then the brainiest, strongest man in the class, whom every one looked up to, said, with an emphasis that made the windows rattle: "Shut up!" And never, through all the rest of that young man's college course, did he hear an unclean thing said in that room. The man who gives himself up to Christ and gives Christ the seat of honor in his heart challenges the devil and whips him every time.

And now comes the solemn, earnest question which you must meet face to face to-night: "What am I going to do with this Christ who is knocking at the door of my heart?" His coming in will mean only joy and blessing to you. If you shut him out, you shut out the greatest happiness that can ever come into your life.

Next to the Cremona violins those made by Jacob Stainer, in the Tyrol, in the early part of the seventeenth century, are considered the best in the world, and bring fabulous prices when one of them is on the market. One of these instruments was sold in 1791 under strange conditions. A German Count had heard a gifted musician play upon a Cremona violin of unusual value, and spared no pains to secure the instrument for himself. He offered enormous sums; but Alessi, the great violinist, said he would sooner sell his life. The rumor of the Count's attempt to get the Cremona went abroad, and some weeks later an unknown old man appeared at the castle door with a worn and shabby violin case under his arm. The servants refused to admit him.

"Tell your master," he said to them, "that heaven's music is waiting at his door."

The Count received him. The old man drew from the unworthy case a perfect instrument, the work of Jacob Stainer's own hand, and played it so marvelously that the Count and his people forgot all about the Cremona. The old man would only sell his instrument on condition that he might pass the rest of his life in the same house with it and play it once daily. And the Count bought it on those terms.

Those are the only terms on which heaven's music can come to your heart. The melodies of divine peace can only be heard in your soul by your opening the door to Christ, who will come in and dwell in your heart and daily sweeten your life with the music of the skies. Do not shut out heaven's music!

Notice the simple conditions—"If any man will hear my voice and open the door." Nobody can fail to know what that means. As Dr. Aitken says, there is no requirement that you shall do any work of cultivation on yourself. Jesus does not say: "If any man make himself moral; if any man will try and make himself better." No, that is not it. "If any man has deep sorrow?" No, that is not it. "If any man has powerful faith?" No, that is not it. This is what he says: "If any man will hear my voice and open the door." But does somebody say: "Ah, faith is so difficult! One man says faith is this, and another says it is another thing?" Do away with such folly! The minute you put your hand out to the door to pull back the bolt; the minute you purpose in your heart to open unto him, and begin to try to obey him by open confession, the bolt will fly back, and he will come in, and there will be joy in your heart.

Do you notice why he wants to come in?—not to have a funeral with you, but to have a feast. He wants to sup with you and wants you to sup with him. Oh, the glad time there may be in your heart to-night if you will let him in!

Now all this study and meditation together will fail entirely unless you actually, definitely, throw back the bolt and let Christ in. A young boy was very eagerly listening to his father as he read the chapter in which this beautiful picture of the text is portrayed. But when the father came to this and read, "Behold, I stand at the door and knock," the eager child could restrain himself no longer, but running across the room to his father, he asked: "Father, did he get in? Did he get in?" Let Christ into your heart now!

XXX.

A DOOR OPENED INTO HEAVEN.

Behold, a door opened in heaven.—*Rev.* iv. 1 (*Revised Version*).

THE famous Dr. Muhlenberg, he who wrote the hymn "I Would Not Live Alway," and was afterward sorry he did it because of the pessimistic note in it, was a great teacher of boys. He used to say that it was a bad sign when a boy engaged in his play received a letter from home and went on playing without stopping to read the letter. This man, who knew and loved boys so well, declared that that was a worse sign than a bad recitation. So it is a bad sign with us when we do not care to hear about heaven and the blessed home which God is preparing for us as his children. It is proper and right that we should be taken up to a large extent with our work in this world; but we ought not to be so frenzied with the competitions and excitements of earth that we shall cease to think about heaven with interest and earnest attention.

Sometimes we hear people talk as tho thoughtfulness about the other world and rapturous contemplation of the heavenly life made men unfit to do well the work which needs to be done here; but such is not the case. It enlarges our vision, broadens our nature, and makes us worthier and nobler citizens of this world to remember that our citizenship is already registered in the skies.

John saw one door opened in heaven at this particular period of his life of which he speaks in our text; but the Bible opens many doors for us. Heaven is described to us under a great variety of pictures. Dr. Dawson Burns gathers a number of these illustrative figures of heaven into a very helpful song entitled "What is Heaven?"

> "Heaven is a Garden, and its soil
>   Luxuriant teems with flower and tree
> Whose nurture claims no care or toil,
>   But all is fragrant, fair, and free:
> In that sweet Garden may we walk,
> And with beloved companions talk!
>
> "Heaven is a City, widely spread;
>   None can its thronging people count;
> Its jasper walls enclose no dead;
>   Life streams redundant from its fount:
> That City all is 'Holy Ground';
> May we its citizens be found!
>
> "Heaven is a Temple, grander far
>   Than eye has seen or fancy paints;
> No blemish can its worship mar—
>   Its ministers are Christ's own saints:
> As lowly ministrants would we
> Its worship and its glory see!

A DOOR OPENED INTO HEAVEN. 259

"Heaven is a Sea of glass and fire,
  Where harpers strike each joyful chord;
And round God's throne the white-robed choir
  Raise grateful songs in full accord:
With harping band, or tuneful host,
Redeeming mercy may we boast!

"Heaven is a Country, out of sight,
  But gained by pilgrims of the earth;
A land of high and pure delight,
  Of blameless peace, and boundless worth:
With loving heart and stedfast mind
That Country we would seek and find!

"But Garden, City, Temple, Sea,
  And Country—these are pictures cold,
And earth-reflected imagery.
  Who would know Heaven must Heaven behold:
Give us, O Savior, by thy grace,
To see our Heaven in thy bright face!"

Let us take a glimpse through some of the doors into the heaven that is promised us to encourage our hearts by the way. The first door we open shows us that it is a roomy place and has "many" mansions. What an idea of largeness and of comfort the Savior has given us in that talk with his disciples which John reports: "In my Father's house are many mansions." One for every soul that yields itself to be God's loving child. When Peter and James and John were on the Mount of Transfiguration, Peter was so overjoyed with the beauty and glory of the revelation of the transfigured Christ in conversation with the glorified forms of

Moses and Elias that he cried out: "Let us make three tabernacles!" But that was not enough. That was not good enough to be true, and so Christ refused him. How much more splendid is the picture of Jesus—"In my Father's house are many mansions." There is room enough for every one who will give his heart to Christ. If there is any one here who has not started his mansion building, start at once. Give your heart to Christ, and he will see to it that your mansion is preparing for you in heaven.

The thought of these new mansions that are being ordered every day by those who confess Christ gives us a glimpse through another open door, which shows us how heaven is changing all the while. Not changing as change is in this world, because it is all the time losing something by decay, but changing in the fact that it is always growing and adding to its beauty and its glory. Christ assures us that heaven is ever new; it will never get old to us. If heaven were like an art gallery, where some of the best pictures were only loaned and were to be taken away soon, one might be impatient to go at once, lest they lose something of the glory. But heaven is like a gallery that is forever receiving new and beautiful pictures, but never one fades or is taken away. It is ever adding to its attractions, and it is never losing anything.

We look through another door, and we see that heaven is a place of blessed reunions of broken fellowships. During the Civil War in this country the news came one day from a Southern battlefield to a New England home that the dear son of that family circle had been killed. In their great grief the family sent directions to have the body sent home, that it might rest in the old graveyard near where the boy was born. And upon the appointed day the broken-hearted father went to the railroad station to receive back all that the war had to return to him of one who left his home in the strength and promise of his young manhood. In his grief the black smoke that rolled away from the engine looked like a funeral pall, as the train slowed up in the station. He looked earnestly for the big pine box, like those which came on almost every homeward-bound train. While he was thus waiting in suspense for the dead, a familiar voice called, "Father!" and in a moment his living son was in his arms. It had all been a cruel mistake, and he was not dead after all. One can easily imagine how much dearer than ever that young man was in his home, receiving him back, as they did, after the fellowship had been broken, as it were, by the sad funeral knell. Heaven shall be full of reunions joyous and glad beyond all our present power to conceive.

Heaven will be a place of appreciation. Loving words are to be said there to the humblest ones by the King in his glory. There is not enough appreciation on earth. We often think we are in too great a hurry for it. It would be a good deal better if we took time enough to say, "Well done!" a great deal oftener than we do. But in heaven every good deed that has gone unrequited here will find its reward. Jesus says that not even a cup of cold water given in a loving spirit shall go unnoticed up there. And what we have done for the poorest and most feeble and unpromising of Christ's brothers and sisters, he will regard and honor as if it were done for himself.

This leads us very naturally up to another open door, which shows us that in heaven age loses its power to make us infirm and weak or to rob us of the faculty of enjoyment. It brings us the glory of immortal youth. A good old man whose life had been infinitely sweet and blessed, but who had suffered from lameness and from many afflictions of the body, wrote with pathos in his sunset years: "There is no ignoring, there is no concealing, the inconveniences which steal over us as we descend into the vale of years. It is a great thing for an old man to retain his faculties and his natural cheerfulness to the last. It is a great thing to keep up his interest in good objects, and in his favorite studies and pursuits. It is a great thing to be surrounded by kind friends and all the endearments and appliances of a happy home; but," said this saint, "greater than all to know Christ, and the power of his resurrection as a hope full of immortality. With this hope he still has something to live for and something to die for." How superior was this man's hope to those words of Cicero: "An old man has nothing indeed to hope for; yet he is in so much the happier state than the young man, since he has already attained what the other only hopes for." What a poor, hopeless state is that compared to the outlook that Paul had when he came to be such a man as "Paul the aged." For him a "crown of righteousness" loomed in sight. For him a "crown of rejoicing" was held in reserve by his Lord. His many burdens and trials seemed only "light afflictions" that were working out for him "a far more exceeding and eternal weight of glory." As his body shivered with the cold, so that he longed for a cloak that had been left by the way, he could still rejoice that, tho the earthly house was being dissolved, he had a building of God, eternal in the heavens.

As we have been looking through these doors into the heavenly world and catching now and then a glimpse, I am sure that our hearts have been thinking of our own treasures on the heavenly shore. God help us to comfort ourselves this day as we think of them, not dead, but living, waiting for us to join them in that land of peace and glory!

No man of modern times has had a clearer spiritual vision than Bishop Randolph Foster. I shall never forget, on one of those days of rare spiritual exaltation which he sometimes reached, hearing him utter what has often been printed, the matchless sentences which portrayed his thought of the condition of the loved ones who had gone on before and of our own reunion with them. With his head thrown back and his face like one in a dream, where the outer eye sees not but the inner gaze is rapt, he exclaimed: "The dead live! In the years gone we had them with us; they became very dear to us. They separated from the throng and gave us their love. They grew into our being, and were a part of us. One day they became weary and sick. We thought nothing of it at first; but morning after morning came, and they were more faint. The story of the dark days that followed is too sad. One dreary night, with radiant face, they kissed us and said good-by. They were dead. Kind neighbors came and carried them out of our home, and we followed with dumb awe and saw them lay them down gently beneath the earth. We returned to the vacant house, which never could be home again. Our hearts were broken. . . . We have searched through the long nights and desolate days for them, but we can not find them; they do not come back. We listen, but we get no tidings. Neither form nor voice comes to us. The dark, silent immensity has swallowed them up. Are they extinct? No. They live. . . . There has been no break in their life. It is as if they had crossed the sea; the old memories and old loves still are with them. New friends do not displace old ones. They are more beautiful than when we knew them, and purer and holier and happier. They are not sick or weary now. They have no sorrow. They are not alone. They have joined others. They think and talk of us. They make affectionate inquiries for our welfare. They wait for us. They are learning great lessons which they mean to recite to us some day. They are not lonely; they are a glorious company. They have no envies or jealousies. They are ravished with the happiness of their new life. They are kings and priests unto God. They wear crowns that flash in the everlasting light. They wear robes that are spotlessly white. They wave victorious palms. They sing anthems of such exceeding sweetness as no earthly choirs ever approach. They stand before the throne. They fly on ministries of love. They are rapturous with ecstasies of love. God wipes away all tears from their faces; and there is no more death, neither sorrow, nor crying, nor any more pain. But why try to describe their ineffable estate? It hath not entered into the heart of man to conceive it. Soon we shall know it all. A day may unfold it. It will burst upon us like a revelation. We shall be speaking tenderly to the weeping ones about us, sorrowful ourselves to leave them, when in a moment, in the twinkling of an eye, the whole scene will change. While the weeping living are yet caressing the still warm clay, the loving watchers will be lavishing their kisses of welcome; not as strangers approaching some lonely shore shall we depart, but as loved and longed-for pilgrims, who return to open arms and welcoming hearts. I long to see Jesus, and angels who have watched over me and befriended me, and all the great and good whose virtues have enriched the ages. I know that I shall hasten rapturously to worship my Lord; maybe he will take me in his arms to bear me over the river, and so to him I shall pour out my great and reverent love; but I am certain I shall see crowding down nearest the shore some forms that will give me their first caresses— forms that will be more to me than all the jeweled host that circle the eternal throne. Heaven will recognize their right, nor will it be for a day."

XXXI.

THE RAINBOW OF MERCY.

And there was a rainbow round about the throne, like an emerald to look upon.—*Rev.* iv. 3 (*Revised Version*).

BACK in the beginning of the Bible, in the first book of the human story, in Genesis, we have the rainbow. From creation it had existed, of course, in the heavens after every rain-storm when the sun shone out upon its retreating phalanx; but God chose it as his pledge to Noah, and to every man that should come after him, that he would never again destroy the earth by flood. It is a beautiful pledge, coming as it always does after a storm; it is like the day which follows night, like the spring that follows winter, like the sunshine after rain; it is God's bow in the cloud which tells us that he loves us as much in storm as in shine.

And now here in the closing book of the Bible, in the midst of the glorious vision which came to this aged Greatheart whom Jesus loved, we have another rainbow. It is the rainbow round about the throne. The throne stands for law. It means government. This picture means that man's salvation is no mere soft-heartedness on the part of God. God's throne is vindicated. Heaven and earth may pass away, but not one jot or tittle of God's law shall fail. God's love does not controvert his justice. God's throne stands forever, and the rainbow is round about the throne because love and mercy are as surely the characteristics of God as justice.

The atonement made by Jesus Christ is not something on the outside, to appease the wrath of an angry Deity. The atonement had its source in God's own heart. "God so loved the world" that he gave his Son. It is strange how men stumble at vicarious suffering in the atonement. We are all well enough accustomed to it in ordinary life. Every mother suffers vicariously for her child. The atonement is God's suffering for man in the person of Jesus Christ on the cross. It is to this thought of God's divine mercy that I want to fasten your attention for a few moments. In that rainbow is the world's hope.

A newspaper man who visited Oberammergau, and who wrote a very brilliant description of the Passion Play, entitled it, "The Story that Transformed the World." But the mere story of Jesus Christ and his sufferings and love could never have transformed the world. It is the great fact deeper than the story, that every sinful man and woman, by confessing their sins and taking Christ as a personal Savior, find their sins forgiven and their hearts cleansed from all unrighteousness, that is transforming the world.

Man was lost, was sick in sin, was without hope; and Jesus came, not only to bring us pardon, but to show us the perfect manhood within our reach and inspire us to rise out of the "mire and the clay," and mount up with wings as eagles into the lofty air of heaven, where we belong.

The story is told that some one gave a gentleman in Scotland an eagle, and he confined it until it sickened. One day he went out and looked at it. It was a pitiful sight. There it was with drooping wings and film-covered eyes. It seemed as if it would surely die. He said to himself: "It is a pity this free bird should die here. I will give it its freedom." He took it out on the heights and put it upon a rock, and went and lay down in the heather to watch what would happen. Presently he saw it lift its head and open its eyes and look. That eagle's eye saw something in the upper air which the man could not see, and that eagle's ear heard something which the man could not hear; but he watched until he saw a speck in the sky, and that speck grew larger, and presently he became aware that another eagle was coming down. Down it swept, with a scream of exultation, and passed over the sick eagle, and fanned it with its mighty wings, and lifted it up upon its own broad pinions, until the sick eagle gathered strength from contact with the messenger from the sky, spread its wings, and soared away into the blue depths. That eagle could bring life and vigor down to earth because it came from the upper air.

Christ came down from the glory of heaven not only to make possible pardon for our sins, and to show us the rainbow of mercy round about the throne, but to fan our faded cheeks with the pinions of his own noble life, to bear us upward on the wings of his courage and faith, and to arouse in us a hungering for the better life for which we were made.

John McNeill tells the story of a man who had a young eagle which he put in the hen-yard with a clog on one of its feet so that it could not fly, and there it grew up. At last, when the man was going to move away from that part of the country, he decided to liberate his eagle. He took off the clog; but the eagle went hopping about just the same among the chickens. So very early one morning he took the eagle and set him up on the coping of the wall just as the sun was rising. The eagle opened his eyes and looked at the sun, and, lifting himself proudly up, stretched his mighty wings, and with one scream of hope launched himself into the upper air, and in five minutes was a vanishing speck.

My dear brother or sister, Jesus Christ has by his atoning sacrifice taken the clog off your foot; he has made it possible for you to be saved. He has made the most beautiful and holy life that was ever dreamed of a possibility for you. But, like that bewildered eagle that went limping about in the dirt after the clog was taken off, you go with your affections running on the earth, with your noble powers chained by your sins, as tho the clog were still on your foot and the life of the skies were not your native breath. I would to God I had power to-night to take you and set you on John's vision-point, where you might with clear eyes behold the sunrise and see the emerald rainbow of mercy about the throne of God.

To have a clear view of that rainbow of mercy is the greatest sight in this world. At a Methodist annual conference a young minister who had made a trip to Palestine was very proud of it; he could not speak on any subject without bringing that in; he referred to it so frequently that it got to be quite a nuisance. At last, after he had been up again, telling what he saw in the Holy Land, Bishop Ames, who was presiding, got up and said: "Brethren, I would rather be five minutes with Christ than to be five years where he has been."

I have only one hope to offer as a way of escape from your sins, and that is the mercy of God in Jesus Christ. I face you with the plain, simple question, "Have you taken Jesus Christ to be your Savior?" I do not ask you how much you know about theology; I do not ask you about your good desires, or about your theories of religion; I ask you plainly and frankly: "Have you laid hold upon the hope set before you in the Gospel?"

Some one tells the story of a philosopher who was crossing a stream. As he entered the ferry-boat he picked up a pebble, and said to the ferryman: "Do you know geology?" The ferryman replied: "No." The learned man said: "Then one-quarter of your life is lost.' As they went on, the philosopher picked up a leaf that was floating in the stream, and said: "Do you know botany?" The ferryman replied: "No." "Then one-half of your life is lost." By and by they reached midstream, and the philosopher, looking up to the starry heavens, said: "Do you know astronomy?" "No, sir." "Then," said the philosopher," three-quarters of your life is lost." Just then the ferryman looked up the stream and saw a wall of water coming down upon them; the dam had burst. He turned to the philosopher and said: "Sir, do you know how to swim?" "No." "Then," said the ferryman, "the whole of your life is lost."

In the great crises of human life theories and excuses are of no value. You will not care about them when you come to die; you will not even mention them at the judgment; only one thing will count then: "Have you taken Jesus Christ as your Savior from all your sins?"

XXXII.

HAPPY WEDDING-GUESTS.

Blessed are they which are bidden to the marriage supper of the Lamb. —Rev. xix. 9 (*Revised Version*)

THERE is something very striking and significant in the figures used in this brief text. There is only one other book in the New Testament where Christ is referred to as the Lamb, and that is in John's Gospel. John the Baptist saw Christ one day, and said to two of his disciples who were standing with him: "Behold the Lamb of God, which taketh away the sin of the world." He had in his thought the mediatorial work of the Lord Jesus Christ. He remembered the references of the old Hebrew prophets to the character and mission of Christ— that he should offer himself as a sacrifice for the sins of the world. The lamb that was slain by the Jewish priest and offered in the temple was a type only, a prophecy of the Christ who should come presenting himself as a sacrifice for the sins of the whole world.

But we have suggested here also a very different figure—that of a bridegroom. For it is to a marriage supper that we are bidden by him who is revealed to us as the Lamb. There is something suggestive in this desire of Christ that his friends and disciples shall think of him in heaven, when he is crowned with glory and power, in the same personality as he was on earth when he suffered and died on the cross for them. Surely it ought to make him very dear to us. It is as tho some strong, brave lover had risked his life in a time of peril and danger to his beloved in order to save her, and in thrusting himself between her and her enemy had brought upon himself grievous wounding. Would it not be true, as he stood at her side at the marriage altar, or sat beside her at the marriage supper, that the scar received in her cause, or the empty sleeve emptied for her sake, would only make him the dearer to her, if she were a true woman? So, surely, it must be with every one whom Jesus Christ has saved and brought into fellowship with himself. The mark of the thorns on his brow, the scars of the nail-prints in his hand, will make him infinitely dearer to us when we shall sit down with him at the marriage supper of the Lamb.

The figure of a wedding-feast used to express the delight and fellowship of heaven is very suggestive and very precious. It pictures an experience of great love and affection. It is love consummated, reaching its climax in marriage. The battles of life are fought and the victory won. All that the devil

The Minimum Christian

[Th]e minimum Christian! And who is he? The Christian who [is hop]ing to be saved at the cheapest rate possible: the Christian [who] intends to get all the world he can, and not meet the world[']s doom; the Christian who aims to have as little religion [as h]e may, without lacking it altogether.

[Th]e minimum Christian goes to church in the morning, and in [the] afternoon also unless it rains or is too warm or too cold or [he is] too sleepy or has a headache from eating too much dinner. [He] listens most respectfully to the preacher and joins in the [pray]er and praise. He applies the truth very judiciously, some[time]s to himself, often to his neighbors.

[Th]e minimum Christian is very friendly to all good works. He [lik]es them well, but it is not in his power to do much for them. [The] Sabbath school he looks upon as an admirable institution, [espe]cially for the neglected and the ignorant. It is not conv[eni]ent, however, for him to take a class. His business engage[men]ts are so pressing during the week that he needs Sunday as [a da]y of rest; nor does he think himself qualified to act as a [teac]her. There are so many persons better prepared for this im[port]ant duty that he must beg to be excused. He is very friendly [to h]ome and foreign missions and colportage, and gives his mite. [He t]hinks there are too many appeals, but he gives, if not enough [to sa]ve his reputation, pretty near it; at all events he aims to.

[Th]e minimum Christian is not clear on a number of points. [The] opera and dancing, the theater and card-playing, and large, [fash]ionable parties give him much trouble. He cannot see the [harm] in this or that or the other popular amusement. There is [noth]ing in the Bible against it. He does not see but that a man [may] be a Christian and dance or go to the opera. He knows [sever]al excellent persons who do. Why should not he? He stands [so cl]ose to the dividing line between the people of God and the [worl]d that it is hard to say on which side he really stands.

[And], my brother, are you making this attempt? Beware, lest you [find] at last that, in trying to get into heaven with a little re[ligio]n, you miss it altogether; lest, without gaining the whole [world], you lose your own soul.—[Presbyterian at Work.

Dr. Dorland.

The Chautauquan Daily quotes Dr. Barnes on this subject the following words:

"The beginning of the investigation was made in an attempt to disprove the much misunderstood so-called Osler theory which, by the way, Dr. Osler says was only a banquet joke.

"The attempt to show the fallacy of the statement made by Dr. Osler was taken up by Dr. William A. N. Dorland, himself a physician and an author of some reputation. He selected the names of four hundred of the most noted men of all times from all lines of activities—statesmen, painters, warriors, poets, writers of history, fiction and other prose productions. Opposite each name was placed the name of the greatest work of his time—his greatest picture, greatest battle, greatest poem or book—whatever the greatest thing he had done in his lifetime might be.

"This list was then submitted to a considerable number of competent critics for suggestions. The list was revised and revised. Names were added, names were dropped; the list thoroughly gone over time and again, until the majority opinion was that the list as it stood represented the four hundred greatest men of the world's history.

"When the list was completed to the satisfaction of the critics, Dr. Dorland appended to the list of the achievements of the men the age at which the deed was accomplished. The list was arranged according to decades of age, and the result was startling. It was found that the decade of years between sixty and seventy contained thirty-five per cent of the world's greatest achievements. Between the ages of seventy and eighty, twenty-three per cent of the achievements fell; and in the years after the eightieth, six per cent. In other words, sixty-four per cent of the great things of the world have been accomplished by men who had passed their sixtieth year; the greatest percentage, thirty-five per cent, being in the sixth decade.

"The figures for the other periods of life are interesting. Between the fiftieth and the sixtieth years are found twenty per cent, between forty and fifty, ten per cent. These all together, leave the almost negligible quantity of one per cent or the world or the flesh has brought against us to separate us from Christ has been baffled and overthrown; and at last we are safely housed at home, and we sit down to a feast of immortal love-life with Jesus Christ our Lord.

It suggests the great joy and gladness of reunion with those that belong to the family of Christ. Who of us has not noticed with pleasure the happy reunions at great weddings, where a large number of guests meet from all parts of the country, and the divided sections of families come together from different parts of the State or nation, and sometimes from across the sea? The occasion is beautified and made romantic and joyous not only by the love which it publicly seals, but by the gladness in the faces of these relatives and friends who look into each other's true eyes again after long separation. But that can only be a feeble type of what the marriage supper of the Lamb will be when all the redeemed and ransomed throng from all lands and all peoples, all purified souls, shall gather as the bride adorned and beautified to partake of the wedding-feast with Jesus Christ, the Bridegroom and Savior.

Who will be there? The whole Bible is an answer to that. Every one who accepts the invitation. All mankind is invited. The invitation is as wide as the human race. No man will be left out in the darkness because he did not receive an invitation. Many times at wedding-feasts in this world there are jealousies and heart-burnings because only a limited number can be invited. But there will not be one soul in all the universe that can say: "I was shut out into the outer darkness because I never received an invitation to attend the marriage feast of Jesus Christ."

Who will be shut out from the feast? The answer is just as plain and simple. Only those who refuse the invitation. It is impossible that they should be there. That they are not there is not God's fault. He does everything that he can do to bring them there. It can only be the fault of the man or woman who refuses the invitation to come. In the Day of Judgment every lost soul will be compelled to say: "It is my own fault." It is not the arbitrary decree of God that a man who will not accept Christ, who refuses his friendship and his mercy here on earth, shall not enjoy the pleasure of heaven. It is simply that in the very nature of things he can not. As Professor Wilder says, "can nots" exist everywhere. We find "can nots" in mathematics. A three-sided square can not be. A four-sided triangle is an impossibility. There are "can nots" in agriculture. You can not gather grapes from thorns, or figs of thistles. There are "can nots" in chemistry. Alkalies and acids can not exist together in peace; they fizz and fuss and boil until the elements neutralize each other. So it is not astonishing that there are "can nots" in the spiritual world. Christ himself has said: "Except a man be born again, he can not see the kingdom of God." These words were not uttered by the Savior to some outbreaking sinner who was in disgrace, but to Nicodemus, an educated and moral man, whose reputation was blameless before the community.

I come to you to-night with the invitation from Christ, and the assurance that if you will come unto him he will not cast you out. If you will begin now to confess him, he will dwell by his Spirit in your heart as long as you live in the world, and when death comes he will welcome you to the great feast of perfect love in heaven. If you are to enjoy the marriage supper, you must yield your heart to his loving courtship and tender fellowship here on earth. A wicked man at the wedding-feast in heaven would find his unhappiness as terrible as tho he were thrust into the deepest hell. If we are to enjoy heaven, we must begin to enjoy the heavenly spirit here. If you will confess your sins to Christ, and acknowledge his love for you, and your engagement to him before the world, he will, day by day, transform your thoughts and affections, so that your heart will beat in harmony with his, and when the heavenly marriage day comes an assembled universe will unite in saying that it is a most proper marriage. Thank God! he is able to do what he promises; and however sinful your heart may be now, if you will surrender it to him he will transform it into his own likeness and image.

Many years ago, when Moody was just beginning the work that has attracted such world-wide attention, he was holding meetings in the West. He was preaching one day on the prairie, when a man drove up in a fine turnout, and after listening a little while put his whip to his horse and drove away. He came back night after night, until Moody saw that he was very much interested. After the meeting one night he inquired: "Who is that man who drives up here every night? Is he interested?"

"Interested! I should think not! You should have heard the way he talked about you to-day."

"Well," the evangelist replied, "that is a sign he is interested."

Moody expressed his determination to go and see him. His friends tried to keep him from going, for they said he would only curse him. But he went. He found him to be the wealthiest man within one hundred miles of that place. He had a wife and seven beautiful children. But he was a great blasphemer. He could not sit down at his table with his family without cursing and swearing. Just as Moody got to his gate he saw him coming out of the front door. He stepped up to him and said: "This is Mr. ——, I believe."

He said: "Yes, sir; that is my name." Then he straightened up and asked: "What do you want?"

"Well," said the evangelist, "I would just like to ask you a question if you won't be angry."

"Well, what is it?"

"I am told that God has blessed you above all men in this part of the country; that he has given you wealth, a beautiful Christian wife, and seven lovely children. I do not know if it is true, but I hear that all he gets in return is cursing and blasphemy."

The man looked astonished for a moment, and then said: "Come in; come in."

They went in.

"Now," the farmer said, "what you said out there is true. If any man has a fine wife, I am the man; and I have a lovely family of children, and God has been good to me. But, do you know, we had company here the other night, and I cursed my wife at the table, and did not know it until after the company had gone. I never felt so mean and contemptible in my life as when my wife told me of it. She said she wanted the floor to open and let her down out of her seat. If I have tried once I have a hundred times to stop swearing. You preachers don't know anything about it."

"Yes," said Moody, "I know all about it; I have been a drummer."

"But," responded the farmer, "you don't know anything about a business man's troubles when he is harassed and tormented the whole time; he can't help swearing."

"Oh, yes," said the preacher, "he can. I know something about it. I used to swear myself."

"What! You used to swear? How did you stop?"

"I never stopped."

"Why, you don't swear now, do you?"

"No; I have not sworn for years."

"How did you stop?"

"I never stopped. It stopped itself."

The farmer said: "I don't understand this."

"No," said Moody, "I know you don't. But I came up to talk to you, so that you will never want to swear again as long as you live." And so Moody told him the old, old story of how Jesus Christ can take the temptation and desire to swear out of the heart.

"Well, how am I to get to Christ?"

"Get right down here and tell him what you want."

"But I was never on my knees in my life; I have been cursing all day, and I don't know how to pray or what to pray for."

But he did get down on his knees and blundered out a few short sentences like the publican's cry of "God be merciful to me a sinner." That night he went to the meeting and stood up and said: "My friends, you know all about me; if God can save a wretch like me, I want to have you pray for my salvation."

Thirty years passed away, and Moody was in Southern California, when this man came to him and told him who he was. The first word Moody said to him was: "Oh, tell me, have you ever sworn since that day you knelt in your drawing-room and asked God to forgive you?"

"No," he said; "I never have had a desire to swear since then. It was all taken away."

Come and give your heart and life up to this same blessed Savior. Let him transform you into his own image and fit you to enjoy heaven with him forever.

XXXIII.

THE GREAT WELCOME.

And the Spirit and the bride say, Come. And he that heareth, let him say, Come. And he that is athirst, let him come: he that will, let him take the water of life freely.—Rev. xxii. 17 (*Revised Version*).

How gracious it is on the part of our Heavenly Father that this Book, which from beginning to end—in history and prophecy and poetry and revelation of spiritual things—has the one great purpose running through all, the salvation of the world through Jesus Christ, should end with this great chorus of welcome to the sinner! In every possible way God has sought in this Book to show men the folly of wickedness and the wisdom of obedience to him. We have seen the flaming sword about the Garden of Eden, and its inhabitants exiled because of sin. We have seen Cain fleeing, a vagabond, in despair; and Abel, tho dead, yet speaking for righteousness. We have seen the world deluged for its wickedness, and righteous Noah and his family saved because of their faith and obedience to God. We have seen Abraham going out, a stranger and a pilgrim, into an unknown land, because his eye caught a glimpse of the city in the skies. We have observed Lot, in his haste to get rich, drifting into Sodom to the ruin of his household. We have seen Elijah's triumph over his enemies on Mount Carmel and Elisha surrounded by the chariots of God at Dothan. We have watched Samson, the mighty, toying with sin until, old and blind, he grinds in the mill of his enemies like a beast of burden. We have seen Daniel a captive in a strange land, faithful to his God in the midst of temptation, growing great and splendid among foreigners, and able because of his righteousness to look a lion out of countenance in his old age. We have heard David sing psalms of faith and confidence in the Divine Shepherd. We have looked through Isaiah's long glass, as he peered down the centuries and saw Christ coming with the Spirit of God upon him to preach deliverance to captives, to open the prison doors to the bound, to preach the Gospel to the poor, and to heal the sorrows of the broken-hearted. We have seen the day of redemption draw near, the wise men coming from the East, and heard the angels sing to the shepherds their tale of good tidings. We have watched the child Christ grow from a babe in Bethlehem till in the fulness of his ministry he could say to the disciples of John the Baptist, who inquired if he was the Messiah: Go tell John what you have seen. The poor hear the Gospel, blind men see, deaf men hear, and the lepers are cleansed. We have followed the Christ until we stood with him under the shadow of the cross and heard his death-cry, while the sun was veiled in darkness. We have gone with the Marys on Easter morning, and stood beside the open grave and its vision of angels. We have heard Peter preach on the day of Pentecost, and walked with throbbing hearts through the early years of Christian experience and triumph until we stood with Paul among the saints of Cæsar's household in Rome. And now, at last, with this aged Greatheart ready for his translation, we have been with him in the spirit on the Isle of Patmos, and heard the wonderful warnings and rebukes, the invitations and promises, from the lips of the angel who was the interpreter of Jesus Christ.

And so we come to the last book in the Bible, and the last chapter of that book, and Christ speaks, bearing testimony to the truthfulness of the angel who has been his interpreter, and we have this great message of welcome.

In every book from Genesis to Revelation we have seen that sin brings sorrow and remorse, that it dwarfs character, that it blights life, that it degrades and debauches and destroys the soul; and, on the other hand, we have seen on every page that righteousness exalts both the man and the nation, that the one thing which endures all the storms of life is goodness, that that which brings a man close to God and makes life sweet and happy is love, that

that which makes life strong and courageous is hope and faith which throw their anchor beyond the channel of death into the harbor of heaven.

These are the messages that have come to us everywhere. And now at the last our Savior who died to redeem us makes one more effort to welcome us so earnestly, so tenderly, so graciously that not one will refuse.

You might compare the Bible to a great musical composition, rising and falling in the sweep of the music, until, near the end, it gathers all singers together in one mighty, overwhelming, irresistible wave of song.

You might compare the Bible to a feast, gathering in richness from the promise of a Savior made to Eve, on through patriarch, and prophet, and poet, and apostles, and angels; a feast ever growing richer and more splendid, until you come to the last, and find that Christ, as at Cana in Galilee, where he wrought his first miracle and where he gave the best of the wine at the last of the feast, has given us here the richest and the most gracious of all the Bible invitations to the hungry, thirsty, needy souls of men.

What a great chorus of welcome it is! The Spirit says, Come. How long that has been true with you! Many a time when the Gospel has been preached faithfully, the Holy Spirit has been true to the promise and has accompanied the word and made you feel your sinfulness, and you have been convinced of the truth of God's message, and have said in your heart: "I ought to yield now." Many a time in the quietness of the night "the still, small voice" has spoken in your conscience; and to-night the Spirit calls again. If you are not saved from your sins to-night, it will be because you sin against the Holy Spirit and refuse to listen to his invitation.

Then there is the voice of the church. The Bride says, Come. To most of you she has been saying it since your birth. Some of you were christened at the altar of the church in your infancy; the church said "Come" to you through the lips of your Christian mother. She spoke to you through the voice of your Sunday-school teacher. The very spire of the building, reaching heavenward, as well as the sermons and hymns, have said "Come" to you all these years. During all this month the lighted windows, the open doors, and the invitations of the church on every hand have been saying "Come" to you. If you are not saved it will be because you refuse the invitation of the church.

Others who have heard the Gospel have said "Come" to you. Every man and woman and child who have heard the Gospel and have come to this altar confessing sinfulness and pleading for salvation have by example appealed to you to come to Christ. If you let this month pass and this last invitation of the month close without being saved from your sins, it will be in the face of all this new testimony to Christ's power to forgive sins.

And now we come directly to the word of Christ to you: "And let him that is athirst come." I am sure that there is not one of you here but will bear testimony, if you are honest, to the fact that there is no real rest to the soul without a consciousness of sins forgiven, and a hope of heaven. Ah, the restlessness of human souls; the thirst of life! How men run to and fro on the earth, pushing one another to the wall in their fierce competition for wealth and fame and pleasure, trying to find something to satisfy the thirst of an immortal soul! I come to you in the midst of this lack of peace with Christ's invitation to come and slake all your thirst in him.

But here is preparation for those who are not conscious even of their thirst: let every man that "will," come. Even tho your conscience does not stir in you; tho your sorrows do not move you; your mind, your thought, your judgment which God has given you tell you that it is right to serve God; that it is the honorable, the grateful, thing to confess Christ; that it is the safe and the true thing to model your life after the life of Jesus. Here is an invitation to you: let every man that "will," come. Every one that will make up his mind to follow Christ in the noblest possible life to be lived in this world: let him come.

And there is no invitation here to a meager supply. All the provisions are abundant. Coupled with every invitation is this last clause, "Let him take the water of life freely."

I was reading the other day Nansen's book describing his crossing of Greenland. For many days and weeks they were never a single waking moment oblivious to an all-consuming thirst for water. They were crossing over the ice, and the cold was so intense that they were only able to heat water enough to have a little tea, and allow themselves the very smallest possible allowance to drink. And so they trudged on painfully day after day, dreaming what it would mean to have enough water to drink. One day, after striking camp, they wandered off a little to prospect their surroundings, when they saw, deep down in a hollow in the ice, at a distance, glistening in the sun, what seemed to be water. They hurried over the ice toward it, and as they became certain that it was indeed water, they pushed forward with the greatest excitement. They threw themselves down on the ice at the edge of the little pool that had been melted by the sun, and drank, and drank, and drank again, until they dared drink no more. Nansen declares that no one who has never experienced it can have any adequate conception of the delicious taste of that water, and of the precious privilege of being able to drink it without stinting themselves.

That is only a faint illustration of what it is when a thirsty soul that has been seeking for peace in worldly or sinful things, and found no peace, at last accepts the invitation of Christ and bows down at the "water of life," and drinks without stint at that immortal fountain.

Come to Christ to-night! President Leonard Woods, when he was at the head of Bowdoin College, was traveling in France, and was invited with others to dine with the king. They presented themselves at the palace, and, entering a large room, went down to meet the king at the other end. The king met them with his accustomed courtesy and said: "We did not know that we were to have the pleasure of your company to-day. You did not answer our invitation." Leonard Woods said: "We thought the invitation of a king was to be obeyed—not answered." That was a very witty saying, and illustrates our attitude, our proper attitude, toward Jesus Christ, our King. Do not wait to theorize or question or answer; but obey the Lord Jesus, and come this very hour and partake of the water of life freely!

Books by ❧ ❧

DR. LOUIS ALBERT BANKS.

Christ and His Friends.

A Collection of Revival Sermons, Simple and Direct, and Wholly Devoid of Oratorical Artifice, but Rich in Natural Eloquence, and Burning with Spiritual Fervor. The author has strengthened and enlivened them with many illustrations and anecdotes. 12mo, Cloth, Gilt Top, Rough Edges. Price, $1.50; post-free.

National Presbyterian, Indianapolis: "One of the most marked revivals attended their delivery, resulting in hundreds of conversions. Free from extravagance and fantasticism, in good taste, dwelling upon the essentials of religious faith, their power has not been lost in transference to the printed page."

New York Observer: "These sermons are mainly hortatory . . . always aiming at conviction or conversion. They abound in fresh and forcible illustrations. . . . They furnish a fine specimen of the best way to reach the popular ear, and may be commended as putting the claims of the Gospel upon men's attention in a very direct and striking manner. No time is wasted in rhetorical ornament, but every stroke tells upon the main point."

The Fisherman and His Friends.

A Companion Volume to "Christ and His Friends," consisting of Thirty-one Stirring Revival Discourses, full of Stimulus and Suggestion for Ministers, Bible class Teachers, and all Christian Workers and Others who Desire to become Proficient in the Supreme Capacity of Winning Souls to Christ. They furnish a rich store of fresh spiritual inspiration, their subjects being strong, stimulating, and novel in treatment, without being sensational or elaborate. They were originally preached by the author in a successful series of revival meetings, which resulted in many conversions. 12mo, Cloth, Gilt Top. Price, $1.50; post-free.

Bishop John F. Hurst: "It is a most valuable addition to our devotional literature."

New York Independent: "There is no more distinguished example of the modern people's preacher in the American pulpit to-day than Dr. Banks. *This volume fairly thrills and rocks with the force injected into its utterance.*"

BOOKS BY DR. LOUIS ALBERT BANKS—Continued.

Paul and His Friends.

A companion volume to "Christ and His Friends," and "The Fisherman and His Friends," being similarly bound and arranged. The book contains thirty-one stirring revival sermons delivered in a special series of revival services at the First M. E. Church, Cleveland. 12mo, Cloth, Gilt Top, Rough Edges. Price, $1.50.

The Christian Gentleman.

A volume of original and practical addresses to young men. The addresses were originally delivered to large and enthusiastic audiences of men, in Cleveland, at the Young Men's Christian Association Hall. 12mo, Buckram. Price, 75 cents.

Hero Tales from Sacred Story.

The Romantic Stories of Bible Characters Retold in Graphic Style, with Modern Parallels and Striking Applications. Richly Illustrated with 19 Full-page, Half-tone Illustrations from Famous Paintings. 12mo, Cloth, Gilt Top, Cover Design by George Wharton Edwards. Price, $1.50.

Christian Work, New York: "One can not imagine a better book to put into the hands of a young man or young woman than this."

The Saloon-Keeper's Ledger.

The Business and Financial Side of the Drink Question. Among the items treated are: The Saloon Debtor to Disease, Private and Social Immorality, Ruined Homes, Lawlessness and Crime, and Political Corruption. 12mo, Cloth. Price, 75 cents.

The Christian Herald, Detroit: "This is one of the most notable contributions to temperance literature of recent years. The discourses are the masterpieces of an expert, abounding in apt illustrations and invincible logic, sparkling with anecdote, and scintillating with unanswerable facts."

Sermon Stories for Boys and Girls.

Short Stories of great interest, with which are interwoven lessons of practical helpfulness for young minds. The stories have been previously told in the author's congregation, where their potency and attractiveness have become surprisingly manifest. The book has a special value for the Sunday-school, the nursery, the pastor's study, and the school-room. 12mo, Cloth, Artistic Cover Design, Illustrated. Price, $1.00.

BOOKS BY DR. LOUIS ALBERT BANKS—Continued.

Seven Times Around Jericho.

Seven Strong and Stirring Temperance Discourses, in which Deep Enthusiasm is Combined with Rational Reasoning—A Refreshing Change from the Conventional Temperance Arguments. Pathetic incidents and stories are made to carry most convincingly their vital significance to the subjects discussed. They treat in broad manner various features of the question. 12mo, Handsomely Bound in Polished Buckram. Price, 75 cents.

Herald and Presbyter, Cincinnati: "The book is sure to be a power for good. The discourses have the true ring."

Jersey City News: "Such able discourses as these of Dr. Banks will wonderfully help the great work of educating and arousing the people to their duty."

Revival Quiver.

A Pastor's Record of Four Revival Campaigns. 12mo, Cloth, $1.50.

This book is, in some sense, a record of personal experiences in revival work. It begins with "Planning for a Revival," followed by "Methods in Revival Work." This is followed by brief outlines of some hundred or more sermons. They have points to them, and one can readily see that they were adapted to the purpose designed. The volume closes with "A Scheme of City Evangelization." It seems to us a valuable book, adapted to the wants of many a preacher and pastor.

White Slaves; or, The Oppression of the Worthy Poor.

Fifty Illustrations. 12mo, Cloth, $1.50.

The Rev. Dr. Banks has made a personal and searching investigation into the homes of the poorer classes, and in the "White Slaves" the results are given. The work is illustrated from photographs taken by the author; and the story told by pen and camera is startling. It should be borne in mind that the author's visits were made to the homes of the worthy poor, who are willing to work hard for subsistence, and not to the homes of the criminal and vicious.

The Christ Dream.

12mo, Cloth, $1.20.

A series of twenty-four sermons in which illustrations of the Christ ideal are thrown upon the canvas, showing here and there individuals who have risen above the selfish, and measure up to the Christ dream. In tone it is optimistic, and sees the bright side of life.

Common Folks' Religion.

A Volume of Sermons. 12mo, Cloth, $1.50.

Boston Journal: "Dr. Banks presents Christ to the 'common people,' and preaches to every-day folk the glorious every-day truths of the Scripture. The sermons are original, terse, and timely, full of reference to current topics, and have that earnest quality which is particularly needed to move the people for whom they were spoken."

BOOKS BY DR. LOUIS ALBERT BANKS—Continued.

The People's Christ.

A Volume of Sermons and Other Addresses and Papers. 12mo, Cloth, $1.25.

New York Observer: "These sermons are excellent specimens of discourses adapted to reach the masses. Their manner of presenting Christian truth is striking. They abound in all kinds of illustration, and are distinguished by a bright, cheerful tone and style, which admirably fit them for making permanent impression."

Heavenly Trade-Winds.

A Volume of Sermons. 12mo, Cloth, $1.25.

From author's preface: "The sermons included in this volume have all been delivered in the regular course of my ministry in the Hanson-Place Methodist Episcopal Church, Brooklyn. They have been blessed of God in confronting the weary, giving courage to the faint, arousing the indifferent, and awakening the sinful."

The Honeycombs of Life.

A Volume of Sermons. 12mo, Cloth, $1.50.

Most of the discourses are spiritual honeycombs, means of refreshment and illumination by the way. "The Soul's Resources," "Cure for Anxiety," "At the Beautiful Gate," "The Pilgrimage of Faith," and "Wells in the Valley of Baca," are among his themes. The volume is well laden with evangelical truth, and breathes a holy inspiration. This volume also includes Dr. Banks's Memorial tribute to Lucy Stone and his powerful sermon in regard to the Chinese in America, entitled "Our Brother in Yellow."

Immortal Hymns and Their Story.

The Narrative of the Conception and Striking Experiences of Blessing Attending the Use of some of the World's Greatest Hymns. With 21 Portraits and 25 full-page half-tone illustrations by NORVAL JORDAN. 8vo, Cloth, Gilt Top, $3.00.

An Oregon Boyhood.

The story of Dr. Banks's boyhood in Oregon in the pioneer days, including innumerable dramatic, romantic, and exciting experiences of frontier life. 12mo, Cloth. Tastefully bound and printed. Illustrated. Price $1.25.

FUNK & WAGNALLS CO., Publishers, 30 Lafayette Pl., NEW YORK.

www.ingramcontent.com/pod-product-compliance
Lightning Source LLC
Chambersburg PA
CBHW030817230426
43667CB00008B/1250